Farms & Foods of Ohio

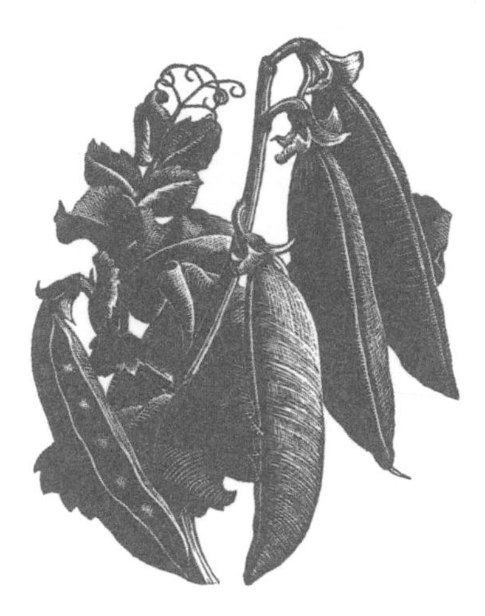

From Garden Gate *to* Dinner Plate

Farms & Foods of Ohio

From Garden Gate to Dinner Plate

MARILOU K. SUSZKO

HIPPOCRENE BOOKS
NEW YORK

Jacket and book design
Christina Matijasic, Edgewater Graphics, Vermilion, Ohio

Production & Typesetting
Dave Crouch, DC Graphics, Brunswick, Ohio

For more information, address:

HIPPOCRENE BOOKS, INC.
171 Madison Avenue
New York, NY 10016
www.hippocrenebooks.com

ISBN-10: 0-7818-1172-4
ISBN-13: 978-0-7818-1172-9

Cataloging-in-Publication Data available from the Library of Congress.

Printed in the United States of America.

This book is dedicated
to family, friends, and farmers.

❦

I am so blessed.

CONTENTS

ACKNOWLEDGMENTS

Perhaps you've heard the saying, "You're only as good as the people you work with." It's true. As I traveled throughout Ohio, I never once met a farmer, family, or chef less than eager to share their story about food and farming.

To that end, I thank all the dairymen, farmers, growers, chefs, bakers, grape growers and winemakers, beekeepers, and maple sugar producers who welcomed me onto their farms, into their barns, and out in their fields. I am particularly grateful for the frequent tastes of farm life—from simple lunches in cozy farmhouse kitchens to glasses of wine sipped in picturesque vineyards.

All in all, it's been quite a ride, all 6,588 miles of it—without a cell phone in tow. Never once did a ringing phone interrupt our conversations because nothing was more important at that time than the person sharing their story.

There were also many agencies and people behind the scenes who offered their assistance throughout this project. Among them are:

- Ohio Fruit Growers Society and the Ohio Vegetable and Potato Growers Association
- Innovative Farmers of Ohio and Ohio Ecological Food and Farm Association
- Christina Matijasic, Edgewater Graphics
- Laura Taxel, a valued colleague
- Tammy Martin, proofreader and Abby Suszko, mapmaker
- Mary Deucher and Margaret Bellis, travel companions
- Recipe Testers: Peggy Artin, Marianne Bodine, Jean Burns, Becky Canfield, Lynda Dolezal, Jennifer Dreschler-Vu, Rachel Friess, Mary Jane Grob, Barb Harris, JoAnn Howley, LuAnn and Justin Jeffrey, Sandy Jordan Kish, Carol Kosik, Trish Kosik, ZoeAnn and Kate Komoransky, Dee Morris, Lorraine Morrison, Liz Niehaus, Dave Ostang, Ann Rich, Fred and Betty Snyder, Jean Staschick, Diane and Rick Tear, Francine Toss, Therese Ward, and Janice Zweigart
- The staff and students at Laurel Run Cooking School, Vermilion

Without a doubt, I am indebted to my family, Ihor, Abby and Ian, for surviving a year's worth of travel and stressful moments as I put these stories to paper. Thank you for knowing when to comfort me and when to leave me be—there's an art to telling the difference.

OHIO

1 Breychaks Blue Egg Farm
2 Buckeye Grove Farm
3 Hartzler Family Dairy
4 Larksong Farm
5 Forrest Family Farm
6 J & K Jacobs
7 Rose Ridge Farm
8 Speckled Hen Farm
9 Freshwater Farms of Ohio
10 Polly's Prawns & Flower Farm
11 Bramble Creek Farm
12 Bridgman Farm
13 Just This Farm
14 Mulberry Creek Herb Farm
15 Oasis Acres
16 The Orchards of Bill and Vicky Thomas
17 Rich Gardens Organic Farm
18 Sage's Apples
19 Schultz Fruit Farm
20 Shafer Produce
21 Sippel Family Farm
22 Franklin's Tall Timbers
23 Integration Acres
24 Killbuck Valley Mushrooms
25 Luers Nut Farm
26 Peace Angel Garlic Farm
27 Queen Right Colonies
28 Windy Hill Apple Farm
29 Firelands Winery
30 Kinkead Ridge Vineyard & Estate Winery
31 Markko Vineyard
32 Ravenhurst Champagne Cellars
33 The Winery at Wolf Creek
34 The Chef's Garden
35 Chez Francois
36 Boulder Belt Farm
37 Alexander House
38 Greenacres Farm
39 Nectar Restaurant
40 King Family Farm
41 Casa Nueva
42 RainFresh Harvest
43 Northstar Café
44 Sticky Pete's Maple Syrup
45 Village Bakery
46 Stutzman Farms
47 Sweet Mosaic

FOREWORD

When Marilou Suszko first contacted me about this book project, I was thrilled with her vision. It was exciting to me because I knew this was a chance to tell stories about Ohio's amazing farmers, people who—often against the odds—are producing the fresh, nutritious, flavorful foods we find at farmers markets and roadside stands, and, increasingly, through subscription farms (CSAs), in restaurants, and in our schools. For all of us, these farmers offer genuine choices about the food we eat. That might be a surprising claim, given the thirty thousand items we find in the average grocery store. But that variety is, in important ways, a fiction. Half of those food items are produced by just ten multinational corporations, a total of roughly 140 individuals sitting on their boards and deciding what our "choices" will be. The farmers Marilou describes here represent real choice—and real food.

They also represent a new breed of Ohio farmers who have adjusted to a landscape that physically, economically, and socially has been transformed in the last half century. Once largely agricultural and rural, Ohio has lost seven million farmland acres in the last fifty years. That's over 350 acres a day, and during the same period at least ninety thousand farms have ceased operation. It's not hard to understand why. In inflation-adjusted dollars, Ohio grain farmers receive the same price for their crop as did their grandparents. Even though total market value of farm products in Ohio has gone up, the distribution of those dollars has skewed: a few farmers receive the majority of those dollars, and many farmers receive the small remainder. No wonder, then, that so many of Ohio's farmers are producing your food on their "second shift," during the evening or early morning hours. As people who eat food, we consumers have had a hand in this as well. Our fast-paced lives have made it harder to pause long enough to prepare a meal with fresh, unprocessed ingredients. If we can be said to "vote with our food dollars" then it is clear we have marked our ballots in favor of the ease and convenience of processed food. When we do that, more of our food money goes to the "middleman" who processes, packages, transports, and advertises food. Of every dollar we pay for our food in the conventional system, about nineteen cents is for the food itself and goes back to the farmer (less than half what it was in 1950). Against this challenging backdrop, this new breed of Ohio farmers is protecting our environment, blazing new pathways to profitability, and providing us the opportunity to connect once more with our place and with each other through our food.

The farmers profiled here give us many good reasons to purchase locally produced foods:

- In the short amount of time it spends traveling from the field and your table, locally grown foods maintain maximum flavor and nutritional value.
- Your support for local farmers helps protect Ohio's farmland: the best way to preserve farmland is to preserve farmers.
- Farmland, in turn, provides important ecological benefits, such as protecting habitat for wildlife and recharging groundwater.
- Buying local foods supports your local economy: it keeps your food dollars circulating among your friends and neighbors.
- Relying on local foods reduces the use of fossil fuels, thus reducing the release of greenhouse gasses, implicated in global climate change.
- And finally, our use of local foods lets us eat in sync with the natural cycle of life, keeping beat with the rhythm of the seasons.

A great advantage of buying your food from the kind of farmer described in this book is that you have the opportunity to find out how your food was grown, see the place where it was grown, and observe for yourself how this benefits the environment and the community. While geographically and agriculturally diverse, these farms have common characteristics: compared to the average Ohio farm these farm operations are smaller—for a vegetable farmer, ten acres is considered large. Perhaps this is why the farmers portrayed here know their land intimately, and this knowledge allows them to carefully protect its natural resources. But if we were to point to a single characteristic that all these farmers share, it is perhaps their willingness to work with nature. Nature herself does not specialize and neither do these farms. From promoting diverse soil micro-organisms to growing many wonderful varieties of a crop, these farmers rely on diversity to nurture their crops, animals, and own souls.

As you meet the farmers in this book, I know you will take comfort and pleasure in entrusting this awesome responsibility to them. Not only do they grow our food but they are cultivating a new kind of food system, one which reflects their own values of environmental stewardship and social responsibility. To them, food is not a commodity but rather a medium for creating communities of mutually supportive farmers and consumer.

Wishing you many good eats.

Dr. Carol Goland

(Dr. Goland is the Executive Director of the Ohio Ecological Food and Farm Association [OEFFA] and an Assistant Professor in the Environmental Studies Program at Denison University. OEFFA was founded in 1979 to promote and support sustainable, ecological, and healthful food systems.)

INTRODUCTION

Let's compare apples to apples.

Buy one apple from the "big box" grocery store near the mall. You know the one. Their produce section is across the aisle from the shoe department. Make note of where you park your car and don't forget to peel the sticker off the fruit hinting it comes from far away.

Now buy the other apple from the farmer down the road, the one who's just coming in from the field with a wagonload of freshly picked apples in tow. "You're just in time," he says and introduces you to an antique variety, Esopus Spitzenburg, a purported favorite of Thomas Jefferson. He gives you a slice of this crisp, scarlet beauty, which he proclaims as "one of the best baking apples around." When you part, he always says, "Thanks, I appreciate your business."

When you get home, put these two apples side-by-side on your kitchen table. Without taking a bite, which apple tastes better?

One is just an apple while the other has charm, personality, and an identity. It's homegrown and a snapshot of what "buying local" is all about. You know everything about it before your first bite—who grew it, who picked it, how far it traveled to get to you, and who your dollar will benefit.

Agriculture in the Buckeye State is big business. Its more than 76,500 farms pour over $79 billion into the state's economy each year and employ one out of seven Ohioans. Nearly half of the state's land, about 14 million acres, is farmland—the majority is used for crop farming and a smaller portion is pasture or woodland. Ohio is a leader in more than thirty-five product sectors, particularly corn and tomatoes.

Yet there is a side to Ohio farming that is more personal. Over three-fourths of Ohio's farms are less than 179 acres, with the majority fifty acres or less. These small family farms are living examples of "sustainable farming"—managed by farmers who depend on the land, in whole or part, to provide a secure living for their families. They are some of the finest stewards of Ohio farmland and models for the rural community, respecting the land, the animals, and the people who buy their products.

You may develop a fondness for a particular fruit, vegetable, meat, poultry, fish, or cheese because it pleases your taste buds. But when you get to know the person whose hand planted the seed, fed the flock or hand-picked the harvest, your fondness easily turns into a passionate pursuit.

There are more than four hundred certified organic farms in Ohio that farm 41,000 acres of wonderful produce, and even more farmers in the state are dedicated to growing or raising their products naturally. Many don't use growth hormones and antibiotics as a matter of routine when it comes to raising meats and poultry, and on their fields chemical fertilizers, herbicides, and pesticides have been replaced by "green" manure, a watchful eye, and diversified plantings. There is a growing dedication to practicing environmentally responsible farming methods in such a way that all living things—animals, flora, fauna, fungi, and insects—coexist peacefully and productively.

Supporting the local farmer makes for good neighbors and builds better communities. There are many chefs putting big effort into finding local growers and producers to stock their ingredient shelves. Building business relationships with farmers encourages a sense of community and an understanding of each other's needs.

Local has many definitions—from around the corner to down the road, regionally or within the state lines, to a much broader definition of personally knowing the farmer or producer who grows or raises what you like to buy. But in essence, "local" is closer to home, where quality, freshness, and flavor is hard to match. And most Ohioans like to eat a little closer to home. More than 75 percent of Ohio consumers prefer to buy Ohio-grown foods. Their enjoyment at the table is enhanced knowing they are supporting Ohio's farms and the local economy.

Now, look inside your pantry or refrigerator—it is filled with more than just food. You'll discover subtle hints about what you find delicious and appealing, your cultural background, ethnic heritage, what makes up the traditions at your holiday table, and your commitment to buying local. Perhaps for you, dining is an event or the opportunity to discover life's really wonderful finds, such as early-season black locust honey, edamame soybeans, pasture-raised lamb, or aged, raw milk cheeses.

Whether you're a cook, a gourmet, or just curious about where your food comes from, this book will take you on a satisfying journey from the garden gate to your dinner plate. Along the way, it will make you more aware, and hopefully more excited, about the gastronomical possibilities rooted in Ohio.

EGGS, MILK & CHEESE

CRACK OPEN A NEWLY GATHERED EGG, pour a tall glass of really cold fresh milk, or nibble on a sliver of handcrafted, farmstead cheese, and celebrate! Many of Ohio's small family farms have turned their flocks and herds back out to pasture to feast on a menu intended by nature—sweet, succulent shoots of grass, tender herbage, and protein-rich bugs—all enjoyed in the warm sunshine and fresh air. Returning to a more natural, simpler way of farming was not a decision made around a conference table but around the kitchen table. While it's still a business, farming in a way that is right for everyone—the animal, the farmer, the land, and the customer—also becomes a lifestyle, placing these farmers among the best stewards of Ohio farmland.

Eggs, milk, and cheese straight from the farm have full, genuine tastes that perhaps you remember from long ago. If you're part of a new generation of cooks and connoisseurs, be prepared for flavors you've never experienced before. When it comes straight from the farm, it's all about flavor.

BREYCHAKS BLUE EGG FARM

Kathy Breychak
Columbia Station, Ohio

The chickens on Kathy Breychak's Columbia Station farm are barnyard Monets. Their nests are filled with a colorful palette of eggs in shades ranging from chalky white to warm cinnamon, seafoam green to bright azure, soft buff to dusky pink, and everything in between.

What began as a hobby of hand-painting eggs intended as ornaments, hatched into a bigger small business for Kathy who named her Blue Egg Farm not just for the blue eggs laid by her Araucana chickens, but for her fondness for the color. "Everything I have is blue, from my car to my dog, Sparkle, a blue merle Australian Shepherd," she says.

Although a talented artist, Kathy noticed that her customers were expressing more interest in buying a dozen eggs than displaying them, so she began adding more hens to the yard. Over a short period of time, she went from tending three hens to a flock of 350 which roam freely to hunt for protein-rich bugs and worms, graze on grasses, clover, and timothy, eat wholesome grain, corn, oats, and calcium-rich, ground oyster shells, preen in the warm sun, and take as many dust baths as they please under guard of the dog, a few cats and some overprotective turkeys.

Breychaks Blue Egg Farm barnyard is a constant parade of pretty chicks and beautiful biddies, a mix of standard and heritage breeds, some unusual and others rare, each laying distinctly colored eggs. The little know Barnevelders are calm and friendly little ladies who lay large, rich reddish brown eggs, and French Marans are trendy birds known for their chocolate-colored eggs. Andalusians are rare, blue-feathered beauties that lay creamy white eggs. Friendly, intelligent Araucanas, with their red earlobes, topknots, and fluffy muffs of feathers that cover their ears, add personality to the yard as well as color to the cartons of eggs Kathy collects. Nicknamed the "Easter Egg Chicken," they lay eggs in deep blues, pastel greens and pinks, olive drab, and an occasional antique gold. Even their chicks arrive in colors ranging from black to brown, red, and white.

Kathy finds people's reactions to a dozen of eggs—her eggs—amazing. "I am always being asked if I colored the eggs or what I feed my chickens to get those colors," she says. While she might get the credit, Kathy quickly educates the customer that from one chicken to the next, the eggs taste the same but the chickens' physiology is responsible for the color of the shells. "The short answer is that breed will determine the shell color," she explains. "The long answer is that as the shell forms in some breeds, it becomes pigmented from hemoglobin to produce brown tones, and in others, by cyanins from bile to produce green to blue shades—or if there is no pigment released, the shells are white." Still, Kathy reminds customers that the color of the shell has no connection to the quality of the contents. "It goes back to how well the chickens eat!"

It might be hard to imagine opening a carton of eggs and feeling excited about the contents if your measure of great eggs is to just find all twelve intact. Farm-fresh eggs will forever change your expectations the first time you crack one open and slip it into a hot skillet. The white remains thick and the fat, vibrant orange yolk stands tall, and the taste is wonderfully fresh, "like butter," compares Kathy. But in her opinion, the real difference between the eggs from Breychaks Blue Egg Farm and those stacked six-deep in the dairy case is that, "I can tell you everything about where my eggs come from."

Raspberry Cream Custard

Custards are great showcases for the rich colors and fresh taste of farm-fresh eggs. You can skip the step of broiling the top, if desired, but plunging your spoon past the crunchy, sugary shell and into the creamy custard will make this dessert feel extra special.

Makes 6 servings

4 fresh eggs
½ cup sugar
1 teaspoon vanilla extract
1½ cups whole or low fat milk
½ cup half-and-half
1 cup fresh raspberries
6 teaspoons coarse sugar, for broiling (optional)

Preheat oven to 325°F. Lightly butter six 6-ounce custard cups.

Place the eggs, sugar, and vanilla in a large bowl and beat until well blended, about 1 minute. Gradually whisk in the milk and half-and-half. Place 6 raspberries in each custard cup. Reserve the remaining berries for garnishing. Divide the egg mixture among the cups. Set the cups in a 9 x 13-inch baking pan.

Place the pan in the oven and carefully pour very hot water into the baking pan, being careful not to splash the water into the cups. Fill until the water reaches halfway up the sides of the cups.

Bake until the custard is just set, 40 to 45 minutes, or until a knife inserted in the center of the custard comes out clean. Let the custards cool completely before removing from the water bath. Discard the water.

When ready to serve, preheat the broiler. Put the custard cups on a baking sheet. Sprinkle a teaspoon of sugar on each custard and set under the broiler, 4 to 5 inches from the heat, and broil for about 2 minutes, or until the tops are golden and bubbly. Garnish with the remaining berries and serve.

Poached Eggs in Red Sauce

Here's a dish that brings together fresh flavors from the field and henhouse. It's great for dinner or brunch served with a simple salad and crusty, toasted bread for soaking up the sauce.

Makes 4 to 6 servings

2 tablespoons extra-virgin olive oil
2 cloves garlic, minced
½ cup chopped onion
½ cup chopped mushrooms
8 to 10 ripe medium red tomatoes, seeded, chopped and lightly mashed to release juice
Splash of red wine (optional)
¼ cup freshly chopped basil or parsley
Salt
Pinch of red pepper flakes
¼ cup heavy whipping cream
6 eggs
Freshly grated Parmesan cheese

Place a large skillet over medium-high heat. Heat the oil and add the garlic and onion, sautéing until soft and fragrant, about 10 minutes. Add the mushrooms and sauté until soft and fragrant. Add the chopped tomatoes and any juices that have accumulated, and a splash of red wine. Cover and reduce the heat to medium. Cook until the tomatoes are soft and have released their liquid, about 20 minutes. Stir in the chopped basil and season with salt and red pepper flakes. Stir in the heavy whipping cream. Crack each egg into the sauce, distributing evenly. Cover and poach until eggs are set, about 5 minutes. Remove from heat and sprinkle with freshly grated Parmesan. Serve immediately.

Sweet Pepper and Onion Flan

Flan is a dish that is all about eggs—fresh eggs! A structural ingredient in baking, eggs provide leavening, color, texture, flavor, and richness to any recipe. They help bind all the other ingredients together, and really fresh eggs expand in the oven, making the flan light and fluffy.

Makes 6 to 8 servings

2 tablespoons unsalted butter
1 medium onion, diced
1 red bell pepper, diced
1 green bell pepper, diced
4 ounces bacon, coarsely chopped
8 eggs
2 cups milk
1 cup heavy cream
¼ cup fresh chopped parsley
Salt and freshly ground black pepper, to taste

Melt the butter in a large heavy skillet over medium high heat. Sauté the onion and bell peppers until soft and translucent, about 10 minutes. Remove and set aside.

Add the bacon and fry until crisp. Remove and drain on a paper towel.

Preheat the oven to 350°F. In a medium bowl, combine the eggs, milk, heavy cream, and half of the parsley. Season with salt and pepper. Pour the mixture into a quiche pan or a 9-inch pie plate, about 2-inches deep. Sprinkle the onion mixture and bacon over the top.

Bake for 15 to 20 minutes until the flan is set. Remove from the oven and let cool for 10 minutes before garnishing with the remaining parsley. Serve immediately.

Chive Blossom Omelet

Making a good omelet is the ultimate test of one's kitchen skills. The tricks are fresh eggs, a light hand and a short amount of time over the flame, which guarantees a fluffy, smooth textured result. Omelets are great dishes for showcasing all types of herbs, but when the purple or white chive blossoms are in spring bloom, they add not only a beautiful look to the omelet but a mild and distinct taste of chives.

Makes 2 servings

2 eggs
1 tablespoon milk
¼ teaspoon salt
Freshly ground black pepper, to taste
1 tablespoon minced fresh parsley
1 tablespoon minced fresh chives
1 tablespoon unsalted butter
6 chive blooms, white or purple, rinsed, dried and carefully separated from the stem

Lightly beat the eggs in a medium bowl. Add the milk, salt and pepper, parsley and chives.

In a large heavy skillet over medium-high heat, melt the butter until it stops sizzling. Pour in the egg mixture. Allow to cook and set undisturbed for one minute. Using a wide spatula, fold one side of the omelet over onto the other and allow to cook for an additional minute or until the center is just set. Slide the omelet from the skillet onto a warmed plate. Sprinkle the top with the chive blossoms. Serve immediately.

BUCKEYE GROVE FARM

Jake and Dixie Scheiderer
Beallsville, Ohio

If you find yourself standing in the middle of the Scheiderer family's Buckeye Grove Farm, take notice of the most amazing lack of sound. Except for the occasional lows of their dairy herd, there's an intense silence, like the kind experienced swimming underwater. "In the morning, you can almost hear the trees breath," says Dixie Scheiderer. "We call that quiet." It's one of the most prominent features on the family's 230-acre dairy farm just north of Marietta. It fits naturally with their desire to "live gently."

Up until the mid–1970s, Jake and Dixie Scheiderer operated a dairy farm in Plain City, just north of Columbus, the fifth generation in their family to do so. "We were part of a big farming community—twenty-three dairies in all," recounts Dixie. The slow creep of urban development began changing the makeup of their agricultural neighborhood. Subdivisions replaced fields where corn and wheat once swayed in the breeze and pastures where dairy cows quietly grazed. "When we go back to visit the old neighborhood, it's like someone took a steel wool pad and scratched it bare," laments Dixie. Feeling squeezed but not ready to give up their farming heritage or the lineage of their Jersey herd, the couple moved east to Monroe County and settled down to milk again amid the lush rolling pastures.

About ten years in, Jake and Dixie approached retirement age. Anyone familiar with the ambitious couple knew that sitting back and watching the world go by was not likely to be the path they would take. Besides, too many things were in place for producing farmstead cheese, handcrafted varieties that reflect the intricate connection between a farm's herd, milk, and the land.

The Scheiderers adopted a "green earth" approach to farming in 1987, which, according to Dixie, "made our herd healthier and left our farm in better condition than when we settled here." Everything they do is to achieve the highest nutritional values in their herd's milk while making a minimum impact on the land and the animals. They run the farm as a "bio-secured" environment, which means that no chemicals, plants, outside visitors, or animals are allowed in the dairy barns or fields. Hormones of any kind are not used to force the cows to produce beyond their natural abilities or for rapid growth.

"Our best crop is the great grass we grow for our cows," says Dixie. "The natural flora grasses and clovers are indigenous to the land, and the 'weeds,' as some folks would call them, provide nutrient-rich herbage for our herd." The milk the cows produce is wholesome, natural, and flavorful, with a butterfat content of about 6 percent, almost on par with rich buffalo milk.

Jake and Dixie are largely self-taught when it comes to making farmstead cheese. They turned to world-class cheese makers in Vermont and Canada for intensive instruction on creating old world varieties such as a mild Hill Folk Jersey and Munsterzilla, a pungent old world French Muenster. They built a licensed production kitchen on the farm where within fifteen minutes of collecting the rich Jersey milk, it's poured into a cheese vat and on its way to becoming one of seven raw milk cheeses.

When Jake and Dixie began making their old-world, handcrafted cheeses, it was with the belief that "if you don't improve and change, you're going to be out." Eventually they would like to "punch" a hole in the ridge running along the southern border of their farm creating a cave, an ideal environment for aging cheeses and developing flavors.

"We may be far off the road most traveled," says Dixie of their farm along an unpaved county road behind a thick stand of trees. "But we know if we are doing something good, people will find us."

Sour Cherry Torte

"If you want to sell cheese, just call it Swiss," jokes Dixie Scheiderer, who learned early in her cheese-making venture that for Buckeye Grove Farm cheese to survive, she would have to gently educate customers to sample and appreciate sharper varieties. Try pairing a thin sliver of a sharp, creamy cheese with the flavor of sour cherries at dessert—they are great compliments to each other.

Makes 8 servings

4 cups pitted sour cherries
2 cups plus 2 tablespoons granulated sugar, divided
3 cups all-purpose flour
1½ teaspoons baking powder
10 tablespoons unsalted butter, softened
2 eggs, lightly beaten
Confectioners' sugar, to dust

Preheat the oven to 350°F.

In a large bowl, combine the cherries and one cup of the sugar. Set aside, stirring occasionally until the sugar is dissolved.

In a separate bowl, combine the remaining sugar, the flour, and baking powder. Cut in the butter and eggs until the mixture is coarse and crumbly. Press half of the mixture in the bottom of a 9-inch spring-form pan. Using a slotted spoon, spoon the cherries on top. Sprinkle the remaining crumb mixture evenly over the top of the cherries and press down lightly.

Bake for 45 minutes, or until the top is golden and the torte shrinks slightly from the sides of the pan. Let cool for at least one hour before slicing.

Just before serving, dust with confectioners' sugar. Serve with a thin slice of sharp, creamy cheese.

Toasted Gouda Sandwich with Pesto and Roasted Red Pepper

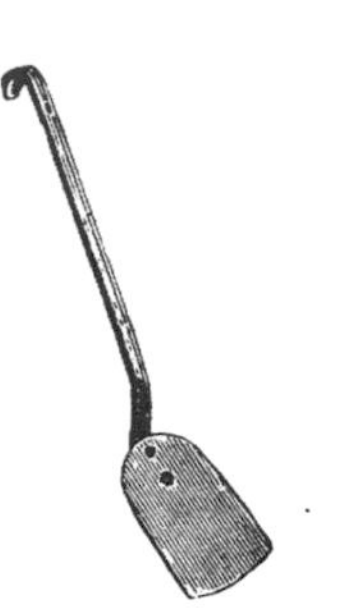

The raw milk cheeses from Buckeye Grove Farm are "farmstead cheeses," made on the farm with milk exclusively from the Scheiderer's Jersey herd. Varieties such as Goudas and Hill Folk Jersey are ripened and matured for a minimum of sixty days. During this time, they develop a wonderfully subtle taste and are sold "young," when a mild flavor, desirable in this recipe, is the goal.

Makes 4 servings

8 slices crusty bread, about ½-inch thick
Extra-virgin olive oil, for brushing
4 tablespoons prepared pesto
2 cups coarsely shredded Gouda or Hill Folk Jersey cheese
2 roasted red bell peppers, halved
Salt and freshly ground black pepper

Brush each bread slice on one side with olive oil. On the other side of half of the slices, spread a tablespoon of pesto and top with ½ cup of the shredded cheese and a roasted red pepper half. Season to taste with salt and pepper, and top with the reserved bread slices, oiled side on top. Press down lightly.

Heat a large skillet or griddle over medium-low heat. Cook the sandwiches 5 to 6 minutes on each side, until the bread is golden and crisp and the cheese is melted. Remove from the heat, cut in half, and serve immediately.

Macaroni and Gouda

In 2004, Jake and Dixie Scheiderer sold the milking operation at Buckeye Grove Farm to their son, Al, and his wife, Renae, who continue to practice the same "green earth" methods, resulting in wonderfully rich nutritious milk and cheeses such as Gouda Boeren Kaas. A favorite variety of cheese-loving Holland, it's seldom found beyond its borders. Enjoy its creamy goodness in this spin on a classic dish.

Makes 8 servings

1 pound small penne pasta or elbow macaroni
½ cup unsalted butter
2 tablespoons flour
1 pound gouda cheese, shredded
1 cup heavy whipping cream, at room temperature
½ teaspoon salt
Freshly ground black pepper, to taste

Cook the pasta according to the package directions. Drain, reserving some of the water. Transfer to a large bowl and cover to keep warm.

Preheat the oven broiler.

Meanwhile, melt the butter in a medium-size saucepan over low heat. Whisk in the flour until smooth. Setting aside ¼ cup of the cheese, add the remaining cheese to the saucepan. Increase the heat to medium and stir for about one minute. Gradually add the cream, stirring constantly. Continue to stir for two minutes until mixture is thick and hot. Stir in the salt and pepper. Remove from the heat and pour over the macaroni, mixing well. (If the macaroni appears dry, toss with a little of the reserved water to loosen before adding the cheese mixture.)

Divide the macaroni and cheese into eight 12-ounce ramekins. Sprinkle the remaining cheese on top. Place under the broiler for one minute or until the cheese is melted and golden brown. Serve immediately.

French Emment, Pear, and Ham Salad With Mustard Seed Vinaigrette

When the cows of Buckeye Grove are on summer pasture, the green grasses store sugars and beta-carotenes, which yield darker cheeses. In the spring and winter, the cheeses are lighter in color and milder in taste because the herd's diet is largely dried grasses. Regardless of the season, Dixie Scheiderer is convinced that milk from Jersey breeds is what makes their French Farm Emment so flavorful. Aged just over one year, its flavor is akin to Swiss, with a little more zip.

Makes 6 servings

Vinaigrette:

¼ cup Dijon mustard
2 tablespoon rice vinegar or champagne vinegar
½ cup extra-virgin olive oil
1½ tablespoons mustard seeds, lightly toasted
Salt and freshly ground black pepper

Salad:

6 cups romaine or Bibb lettuce, washed and torn into bite-size pieces
2 firm red pears, cored and cut into thin slices
12 ounces Black Forest ham or smoked ham, cut into thin strips
12 ounces French Emment cheese, cut into thin strips
½ cup walnuts or pecans, lightly toasted
Salt and freshly ground black pepper, to taste

Chill six salad plates. In a small bowl, whisk together the mustard and vinegar. Add the olive oil in a slow, steady stream, whisking constantly. If the dressing is too thick, add a little water. Stir in the mustard seeds and salt and pepper to taste.

In a large bowl, toss the lettuce, pears, and ham with the vinaigrette. Divide the mixture between the chilled salad plates. Top with the cheese and nuts. Lightly season with salt and pepper. Serve immediately.

HARTZLER FAMILY DAIRY

The Hartzler Family
Wooster, Ohio

When Harold Hartzler was growing up on the family farm in the 1930s, his sister Lois would make a game out of walking behind their father's plow, picking up the earthworms unearthed by the blades. What was once a game later became a revelation for this career dairy farmer. Thirty years later, Harold was plowing the same fields, as he had been doing for the better part of his life. Like his sister, he began to look for worms in the tilled earth but he didn't find any. He couldn't help but wonder why the worms didn't want to live in this dirt.

The Hartzler farm, like most dairy farms at that time, used chemicals to control pests and disease. Herbicides washed off during a rain would run off into another field where hay was grown to feed the herds. Sometimes the hay would die. Harold Hartzler, now the family patriarch and father to eight future dairy farmers and workers, knew it was time to make some decisions about the way his family would continue to farm. So in 1964, he began to reverse the trend and worked to restore a healthy balance to the Hartzler farm and herds. He began composting weeds and rotating feed crops, such as corn and oats, with nitrogen-rich cover crops to revive the soil and restore nutrients. He began to notice that this improved soil environment invited the worms back but kept away the pests that found healthy plants and corn too much of a challenge.

Today, the Hartzler dairy and herds are used as a model by the Ohio Agricultural Research and Development Center for other dairy and produce farmers around the world. Although not certified organic, Hartzler's natural farming methods improve the health of the soil and the plants and, in turn, the health of the herd, their milk, and, ultimately, the Hartzler customers.

"The people who drink our milk, eat our ice cream, and use our butter long to get back to where their food comes from, and they want to eat right," says daughter Janis, whose job at the family dairy is to meet and greet the public, and host tours of the dairy. "We get rid of anything complicated in our milk products and get back to the basics."

The dairy's herd of 250 Holstein and Jersey breeds produces about four thousand gallons of milk a week, which is processed into whole, skim and 2 percent styles and chocolate milk that tastes and pours like liquid ice cream. As with everything good, the cream rises to the top. Hartzler milk is not homogenized, a process that prevents the cream from separating from the rest of the milk, but gently pasteurized to maintain the integrity of flavor and nutritional quality of the milk. "The more you process, the less you have to enjoy," says Janis, who describes the taste of Hartzler milk as "sweet with a caramelized flavor."

To preserve that taste, all their milk is bottled in glass. "We like to think of our milk as winemakers think of wine," she says. "It belongs in glass to stay purer and colder." The thick glass half gallons are refillable, and an old-fashioned "return for deposit" has about 98 percent of the bottles finding their way back to the dairy.

"It's an ongoing challenge to educate our customers on how milk is supposed to taste," says Janis. "That taste is a sensation that may have escaped many milk drinkers in the current generation."

Hot Milk Cake with Roasted Strawberries

This recipe for Hot Milk Cake has been served at the Hartzler family gatherings for years. It's perfect served with fresh strawberries, and outstanding when the berries are roasted.

Makes 8 servings

2 quarts strawberries, washed, patted dry, and hulled
½ cup sugar
10 tablespoons unsalted butter
1¼ cups whole milk
4 eggs
2 cups sugar
2¼ cups all-purpose flour
2¼ teaspoons baking powder
1 teaspoon vanilla extract
Lightly sweetened whipped cream (optional)

To roast the strawberries: Preheat the oven to 400°F. Toss the strawberries with the ½ cup of sugar to coat. Arrange in a single layer in a shallow roasting pan. Roast for 15 minutes, shaking pan halfway through the roasting time. Remove from the oven and let sit at room temperature.

Reduce oven temperature to 350°F.

To make the cake: Butter and flour a 9 x 5-inch loaf pan. Gently heat the butter and milk in a saucepan until the butter is melted. Set aside. Crack the eggs into a mixing bowl. Beat at high speed until thick, about 5 minutes. Gradually add the 2 cups of sugar and mix on medium speed for 2 minutes. In a separate bowl, whisk together the flour and baking powder. Add to the egg mixture and beat until smooth, about 2 minutes. Add the vanilla and the milk mixture to the batter, and mix on medium speed until blended, about 2 minutes. Pour the batter into the prepared loaf pan and bake for 35 to 40 minutes. Let rest for 10 minutes before turning out of the pan. Let cool completely before slicing.

Serve with the roasted strawberries and whipped cream, if desired.

Buttery Shortbreads

One of the best ways to showcase the sweet taste of naturally sweet, pure butter is in a true shortbread cookie. Simple to make, they only require three ingredients: butter, flour, sugar—and a light touch. Minimal handling of the dough will reward you with a finely pored cookie that has a tender, crumbly texture—the perfect cookie for any holiday.

Makes about 2 ½ dozen

1 pound chilled unsalted butter (4 sticks), cut into ½-inch pieces
½ cup sugar
2¼ cups all-purpose flour
Coarse sugar for sprinkling

Position one rack in the middle of the oven and another just above it. Preheat the oven to 300°F. Line two baking sheets with parchment paper.

Place the butter and sugar in a large mixing bowl. Using an electric mixer, cream the ingredients together on low speed for 2 minutes. The mixture will not look smooth. Add the flour all at once and mix on low speed for 3 minutes. The dough will feel soft and sticky.

Turn the dough out onto a floured board and roll out to ¼-inch thickness. Cut out shapes with cookie cutters and transfer to the baking sheets, leaving an inch between cookies. Gather the scraps, roll out, and cut a second time.

Place the baking sheets in the oven and bake the cookies for about 45 minutes, rotating the sheets every 15 minutes. The cookies are done when tops appear dry, not cracked. Transfer to wire racks and let cool completely before storing in an airtight container, or freeze for up to a month.

Milk-Braised Pork

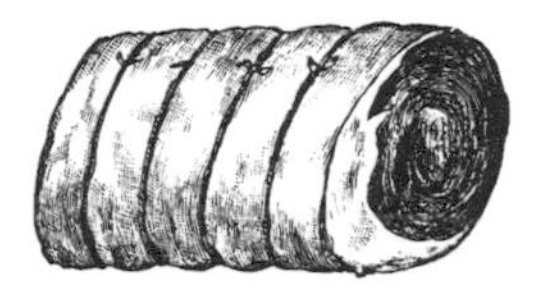

Tougher, economical cuts of meat such as pork shoulder are perfect candidates for milk-braising, a long, slow cooking method that infuses the meats with rich flavor. Don't be put off if the braising liquid appears curdled. When pureed, it creates smooth, silky, flavorful gravy that gives new meaning to "comfort food."

Makes 6 servings

1 boneless pork shoulder (about 2½ pounds), rolled and tied (do not trim fat)
Salt and freshly ground black pepper
2 tablespoons vegetable oil
1 medium onion, diced
1 carrot, minced
1 stalk celery, minced
2 cloves garlic, minced
2 cups whole milk
1 bay leaf
2 sprigs fresh rosemary

Pat the pork dry with paper towels. Season with salt and pepper. Heat the oil in a large Dutch oven over medium-high heat. When hot, add the pork and brown evenly on all sides, about 2 minutes per side. Remove to a platter and keep warm.

Add the onion, carrot, and celery to the Dutch oven and sauté for about 5 minutes, until soft. Add the garlic and sauté for another 2 to 3 minutes. Return the pork to the Dutch oven. Add the milk, bay leaf, and rosemary. Bring to a boil, then reduce heat to a bare simmer. Cover and cook for 2 hours. Remove the lid and continue to cook for an additional 30 minutes. The pork should be very tender when pierced with a fork.

Preheat the oven to 400°F. Remove the pork from the braising liquid and place on a baking sheet. Place in the oven for about 10 minutes until the surface appears dry. Remove from the oven and cover with foil to keep warm.

Meanwhile, return the braising liquid to a boil and let it reduce to about 1½ cups, about 10 to 15 minutes. Remove the bay leaf and rosemary sprigs. Puree the liquid in a blender or food processor until smooth. Season to taste with salt and pepper. When ready to serve, cut the pork into thin slices and serve with the milk gravy.

White Hot Chocolate

Before you uncap a bottle of Hartzler Family Dairy whole milk, be aware that you'll be greeted with a plug of thick cream that has risen to the top, a wonderful feature that adds an incomparable creaminess to hot chocolate recipes. This version is simple yet decadent and meant to be enjoyed during the holidays in the company of family and friends.

Makes 8 to 10 servings

1 cup heavy cream
3 cups whole milk
6 ounces white chocolate, chopped
½ teaspoon vanilla extract
Sweetened whipped cream
Chocolate shavings or sprinkles (optional)

Heat the heavy cream and milk in a large saucepan over medium heat until hot but not boiling, about 5 minutes. Add the chopped white chocolate and stir until melted. Whisk in the vanilla. Continue to whisk until thick and foamy. Pour into individual cups. Garnish with a dollop of whipped cream and sprinkle with chocolate shavings or sprinkles, if desired.

Big Blueberry Muffins

In this recipe, equally important as the quality of ingredients—fresh butter, eggs, and milk—is the added step of placing the batter in the refrigerator for two hours before filling the muffin tins. You'll be rewarded with big, beautiful muffins with crispy, crunchy bakery-store crowns that beg to be eaten first.

Makes one dozen

6 tablespoons unsalted butter
5 large eggs
½ cup whole milk
3½ cups sifted all-purpose flour
2 tablespoons plus 1 teaspoon baking powder
¾ cup granulated sugar
⅛ teaspoon salt
1½ cups fresh blueberries
Coarse sugar for sprinkling

Line a 12-cup muffin tin with paper muffin cups or coat the cups of the tin with cooking spray. Preheat the oven to 400°F.

Melt the butter in a small saucepan over medium heat. Set aside to cool. In a large mixing bowl, beat the eggs until well blended, about 2 minutes. Add the melted butter and the milk.

In a separate bowl, combine the flour, baking powder, sugar, and salt. Add to the egg mixture and mix until just blended, less than one minute. Fold in the blueberries. Cover the bowl with plastic wrap and refrigerate for 2 hours.

Spoon the batter into the prepared baking cups so that it mounds about ½-inch above the top of each cup. Sprinkle the tops with coarse sugar. Bake for 25 to 30 minutes, or until the tops are golden brown. Remove from the oven and let cool before removing from the pan.

LARKSONG FARM

David Kline & Family
Fredericksburg, Ohio

It's the middle of February and David Kline rises at 4:30 A.M., as he does every day of the year. As he walks to the barn where his herd of forty Jersey dairy cows huddle together awaiting the first milking, the snow crunches and squeaks beneath his boots. It's a crystal clear Ohio midwinter morning, the kind where a deep breath of subzero air makes the lungs tingle and the eyes water. There's delight in this moment for David that others might find hard to imagine amid the frigid darkness. To the north, David spots Sirius, the Dog Star, the one that shines brightest in the night sky just before dawn. For this hardworking Amish dairy farmer, it signals the beginning of another great day he'll measure not by the endless chores but in the simplest pleasures that arrive throughout the day.

For David and his wife, Elsie, and their family of five adult children, all married with young families, farming has always been more than just work. "It's fine entertainment and an education," says David. That's not to say that putting up a thousand bails of hay in ninety-degree weather when the breeze has died isn't hard work. "When we look at our work stacked up like neat building blocks in the barn, we realize our profit" he observes. "But the best part is eating homemade ice cream afterward." David calls these "slow-speed pleasures," simple moments of great enjoyment dotted throughout a busy day—like a midday meal of freshly picked sweet corn dripping in churned butter and washed down with a glass of fresh, cold milk.

The Kline's Holmes County farm spans 120-acres where they grow mostly hay and corn, and milk forty Jersey cows to supply Organic Valley, a farmer-owned national cooperative for organically raised dairy, meat, and soy products. The Klines practice an intensive grazing method, which allows the herd to graze as long as the season lets them on a series of pastures, a method that fits the standards of the Organic Valley co-op and respects David's farming philosophy. "Letting our herd graze naturally gives us more leisure time and good-quality milk," he says. "Without it, we would be making big investments in feeding the herd and grooming the pastures. Going back to the old methods lessens our workload."

David and Elsie rely on their own physical power to keep the farm running, but count on the help of family and their Fredericksburg Amish neighbors when the workload demands extra hands. The Amish lifestyle follows a path that emphasizes humility, family, community, and independence from technology. "When you restrict technology, you build community," says David. "One of the best pieces of equipment we have is a horse. They don't have internal combustion engines so our voices don't have to shout over one. As we work in the fields we talk all along." It's a farming style that allows for knowing your children and your neighbors without shouting over the din of a motor.

David relies on nature to track the passing of time and the approaching seasons. He knows that the first monarch butterfly arrives sometime between the seventh and tenth of June. Bright yellow squash blossoms welcome August. "Sounds begin to carry a greater distance at the beginning of September as the trees shed their leaves," says David. Winter gives way to open spaces and a chance to study the land David and his family have just worked for the past eight months. For David Kline, every day he farms is filled with hard work punctuated with a fresh revelation on life or a new observation on nature.

"What gets us through any task on the farm is knowing they are largely seasonal in nature," says David. Shocking oats in August is one of the most intense and least loved chores on Larksong Farm. It requires hand-bundling stiff shafts of oats into sheaves, then leaving them to stand and dry in the field. This is drudgery. "It will only take a few days and then it will be done until next year. It's not like working in the steel mills for forty years. Here everything changes by the day, week, month, year, and season."

Fresh Homemade Yogurt

The Klines enjoy their product at their own table, using their pure, fresh milk for a homemade yogurt that is smooth, silky, and easy to master. Whole milk produces a thicker consistency, but if you opt to use reduced-fat versions, you will notice more water separated from the finished product. Simply drain this off before using.

Makes 4 cups

4 cups organic milk (whole, 2 percent or low fat)
3 tablespoons organic yogurt starter (a good-quality yogurt with active cultures will do)

Pour the milk into a very clean, heavy-bottomed saucepan and place over medium heat. Gently heat the milk until it reaches 185°F when tested with an instant-read thermometer. Remove from the heat and allow to cool at room temperature until the thermometer reads between 105°F and 115°F. Whisk in the yogurt starter. Pour the mixture into a clean, sterilized quart jar with a tight-fitting lid. Wrap the jar in a thick towel and set aside for at least 6 hours or overnight. Remove the towel and place the jar in the refrigerator to chill. To serve, mix with honey or maple syrup, fruit, or vanilla extract. (Use within 2 weeks.)

Chilled Blueberry and Yogurt Soup

Working in the fields provides plenty of opportunity for observing nature and hatching great ideas. Farming Magazine *is a result of long conversations between David and Elsie Kline, who created the quarterly publication. The recipes featured in each issue celebrate the season, such as this one for a chilled summer soup to cool the body down during hot summer days.*

Makes about 6 cups

4 cups fresh blueberries
1 cup water
½ cup honey
2 tablespoons lemon juice
¼ teaspoon ground cinnamon
¼ teaspoon ground cloves
2 cups plain yogurt, plus extra for serving
Fresh mint leaves (optional)

Combine the blueberries and water in a large saucepan. Bring to a boil over high heat and boil for 3 minutes. Remove from the heat, and when cool enough to handle, run through a food mill to remove the skins, or puree in a food processor until smooth. Return to the saucepan and add the honey, lemon juice, cinnamon, and cloves. Bring to a boil again and then reduce heat to low. Cover and simmer for five minutes. Remove from heat and cool to room temperature. Once cool, whisk in the yogurt and refrigerate until well chilled. To serve, ladle into bowls and top with a dollop of yogurt and a fresh mint leaf, if desired.

Yogurt Sesame Bread

David Kline is the author of two books, Great Possessions: An Amish Farmer's Journal *and* Scratching the Woodchuck *(University of Georgia Press), both of which provide a glimpse of his lifestyle through simple detail, poignant notes on nature, and chronicles of simple pleasures such as how the aroma of freshly baked bread can stir the appetite. Using yogurt in this recipe results in a soft, silky dough and tender crumb.*

Makes 3 loaves

2 teaspoons sugar
1 package active dry yeast (not quick-rise)
¼ cup warm water (105°F–115°F)
1 cup (8-ounces) plain yogurt, at room temperature
½ cup unsalted butter, melted and cooled
½ teaspoon baking soda
½ teaspoon baking powder
½ teaspoon salt
3 to 3½ cups all-purpose flour
1 egg, beaten with one tablespoon water
¼ cup sesame seeds (optional)

Dissolve the yeast and sugar in the warm water. Let sit for 5 minutes, then blend with the yogurt, butter, baking soda, baking powder, and salt. Stir in the flour until a soft dough forms. Turn out onto a lightly floured surface and knead for about 5 minutes, until soft and smooth. Cover and let rest for 10 minutes.

Divide the dough into three equal portions. Shape into round or oblong loaves and place on a lightly greased baking sheets. Cover loosely with plastic wrap or a slightly damp linen towel and let rise for about 30 minutes, until about doubled in size.

Preheat oven to 350°F. Lightly brush each loaf with the egg wash. Sprinkle with sesame seeds, if desired. Bake for 35 to 40 minutes, until golden brown. Allow the breads to cool before slicing.

MEATS & POULTRY

"GRASS FED" AND "PASTURE RAISED" are catchphrases earning a lot of well-deserved attention in agricultural and culinary circles throughout Ohio and the nation. While it sounds like something new and cutting edge, it is, in reality, a welcome return to farming the old-fashioned way—without the aid of growth hormones or antibiotics and living on healthy soils, high-quality grasses, often supplemented with wholesome grains and corn. It demands a hands-on approach and requires more than just knowledge and skill.

It also takes patience. When a farmer makes the commitment to raise flocks and herds on grass and natural feeds, it often takes twice as long for the animals to arrive at their optimal market weight. Patience pays off in meats and poultry that are rich and robust in flavor, finely textured, naturally tender and juicy, and distinctively delicious.

While these dedicated farmers represent only a small fraction of producers in Ohio, a state that ranks tenth among the top producers of meat and poultry, they enjoy an exclusive reputation for providing the diversity we crave and seek out in our foods.

Forrest Family Farm

J & K Jacobs

Rose Ridge Farm

Speckled Hen Farm

FORREST FAMILY FARM

Nick Forrest
Oxford, Ohio

There was a time when people harbored the notion that fresh produce or meats that had traveled a great distance to get to their local grocery were more appealing or better tasting than something labeled "homegrown." Apples from Washington State, tomatoes from California, grapes from Chile, strawberries from Florida, or beef from the Longhorn State somehow felt more exotic than what you could get just down the road.

Particularly troubling to Nick Forrest was the perception that lamb from New Zealand was superior to the lamb he was raising on five acres of rich, pastured farmland just outside of Oxford. "There's a big difference between New Zealand lamb and the lamb I raise," he says. "About eleven thousand miles of a difference, to start." It can be as long as two months before New Zealand lamb makes the journey across the Pacific and the United States to get to an Ohio dinner plate.

That distance is one issue to challenge, but Nick also knows there are a lot of skeptics who still confuse lamb with mutton, a mindset perpetuated since World War II, when the tough, stringy meat from older sheep, often two years or more old, although easy to find and inexpensive, was poorly prepared. It literally left a bad taste in people's mouths. Lamb, however, is the meat from sheep less than a year old, often even younger than that. "Their meat is leaner and very tender because tough muscle hasn't had a chance to develop yet," Nick explains.

Since that time, the country's lamb producers moved away from harvesting meat from sheep largely bred for their fine wool, and began raising breeds more desirable for meat, such as Suffolk, Hampshire, and Dorset, descendents of English breeds. For his herd, Nick finds that with good breeding, a natural diet on rich pasture, along with corn, soy, and oats, devoid of growth hormones or antibiotics, his lambs reach market weight quicker and yield more meat-to-bone ratio, especially in the loin, chops and leg areas. "When our lambs go to market, they weigh about fifty-five pounds (dress weight)," he says. "Imported lambs from New Zealand and Australia usually don't get any bigger than forty pounds. We call the chops from those lambs, 'lollipop chops'—it's like an appetizer rather than a main course."

For a long time, Nick found himself using words to describe the wonderful taste of lamb to potential customers and hardened cynics, but found it hard to win most over with a narrative about taste. So he and his wife, Kathy, began to take their product on the road, so to speak, in what they call the "Lamb Road Show." About five or six times a year, the Forrests find themselves in home kitchens with captive, curious audiences wanting to know more about lamb. "It's kind of like a Tupperware party, only with lamb," he jokes. For a few hours, they deliver a primer on lamb: buying, selecting cuts and cooking techniques that include broiling, roasting, sautéing, barbecuing, stir-frying, and stewing. They demonstrate how lamb, served rare to medium, is at its tender, most flavorful best, and how overcooking, a common mistake, can diminish its delicate flavor and texture.

Surprisingly, some of their most eager students also happen to be local lamb producers, colleagues raising great lamb yet without any idea of how to prepare or serve their product. "How were they going to get people to try their lamb if they didn't know the taste themselves?" he wondered. So the Forrests, in a pay-it-forward gesture, educate the producers, who in turn educate their customers, who serve it to their families. It's perhaps a roundabout way of getting their message across, one palate at a time, but when it comes to farm-raised foods, taste speaks so much louder than words.

Italian Leg of American Lamb

Nick Forrest has been a lamb producer for over eighteen years. It began when two of his seven children wanted to show ewe lambs at the country fair. "They kept bringing their projects back home, which turned into a small flock," explains Nick. Before he knew it, the Forrest Family Farm was formed in Oxford. This recipe is one that wins over many trying lamb for the first time with great taste and ease of preparation.

Makes 6 servings

2 cloves garlic, minced
¾ cup grated Parmesan cheese
½ cup extra-virgin olive oil
3 tablespoons chopped fresh basil
1 (4 to 4½ pounds) American leg of lamb, boned, rolled and tied

In a small bowl, combine the first four ingredients to make a paste. Rub the paste on the lamb and place it into a cooking bag. Marinate overnight in the refrigerator.

Preheat the oven to 350°F. Leave the roast in the cooking bag and place it in a roasting pan. Roast in the oven for an hour, or until an instant-read thermometer inserted into the thickest portion of the leg registers 135°F for medium rare. Once the meat reaches the desired temperature, remove from the oven and open the cooking bag. Let the meat rest for 10 minutes before slicing thinly.

Beer-Braised Lamb Shanks

"There are three and a half thousand Ohio producers tending small flocks of forty lambs or less," says Nick Forrest, who also serves on the American Lamb Board. "That's close to half of the total number of producers in the entire country." Lamb, once thought to be spring meat, is raised year round in Ohio, ready in the summer for chops on the grill or meaty shanks for the winter table.

Makes 6 servings

6 meaty lamb shanks
Salt and freshly ground black pepper
¾ cup all-purpose flour
½ cup vegetable oil
1 medium onion, cut into large dice
2 whole carrots, peeled and cut into 1-inch pieces
2 stalks celery, cut into 1-inch pieces
3 tablespoons tomato paste
3 cups amber ale-style beer
3 cloves garlic, crushed
6 cups veal or beef stock
1 whole bay leaf
1½ teaspoons black peppercorns, crushed
2 sprigs fresh thyme
3 tablespoons coarsely chopped parsley

Preheat oven to 350°F. Season the lamb shanks liberally with the salt and pepper. Dredge in the flour, shaking off the excess.

Heat half the vegetable oil in a large Dutch oven over medium-high heat. Add half of the shanks and brown evenly on all sides, 2 to 3 minutes per side. Remove and cover to keep warm. Repeat with the remaining oil and shanks.

Add the onion, carrots, and celery to the pot, and sauté until soft and translucent, 10 to 15 minutes. Add the tomato paste and cook, stirring constantly, until paste darken, about 5 minutes. Add the beer, garlic, stock, herbs, seasonings, and shanks. Cover and bake for 1½ to 2 hours, until the shanks are tender, turning occasionally.

Remove the shanks from the braising liquid, cover, and keep warm. Strain the liquid into a saucepan. Skim off some of the fat and bring the liquid to a boil. Reduce by half, about 15 minutes. Place the shanks back in the pot to keep warm. Serve with Corn Spoonbread (page 39).

Corn Spoonbread

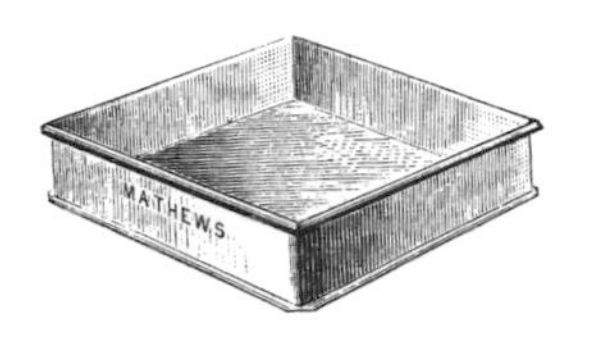

Spoonbread is a soufflé of cornbread, but the term shouldn't scare you from trying this recipe. It's a much lighter version of cornbread and is wonderful with lamb or ham—or even for breakfast with a couple of strips of crispy bacon.

Makes 6 servings

2 teaspoons vegetable oil
2½ cups whole milk
2 tablespoons unsalted butter
1 teaspoon salt
¾ cup medium-grind cornmeal
⅓ cup half-and-half
3 large eggs, separated
1 cup corn, fresh or canned (drained)

Preheat oven to 350°F. Oil the inside of an 8-inch square baking dish.

In a large saucepan, combine the milk, butter, and salt. Bring to a boil over medium-high heat, stirring occasionally. Whisk in the cornmeal in a steady stream and continue to stir until the mixture thickens. Remove from the heat; transfer to a mixing bowl and cool at room temperature for 5 minutes. Gradually add the half-and-half. Stir in the egg yolks.

In a large mixing bowl, beat the egg whites until medium peaks form. Add the egg whites into the cornmeal mixture in three separate additions, gently folding to create a light batter. Gently stir in the corn.

Pour the mixture into the prepared pan and bake until tester comes out clean, 45 to 50 minutes. Cool at least 5 to 10 minutes before slicing.

Mustard and Herb-Crusted Rack of Lamb

The sweet, tender meat of a rack of lamb is the paragon of fine dining. Whether it is a great success or a complete failure is all wrapped up in the degree of doneness. Naturally, undercooking should be avoided completely, but overcooking can make the meat dry and tough.

Makes 6 servings

2 racks of lamb, 2 or 3 ribs per portion
1½ teaspoons salt
½ teaspoon coarsely ground black pepper
2 tablespoons extra-virgin olive oil
¼ cup whole-grain mustard
1 teaspoon prepared horseradish
½ cup coarse fresh bread crumbs
1 tablespoon chopped fresh parsley

Preheat the oven to 400°F. Season the racks of lamb with salt and pepper. Place the oil in a large skillet over high heat. Quickly sear the meat on all sides until brown. Remove from the skillet, cover, and set aside.

In a small bowl, combine the mustard and horseradish. In a shallow dish, combine the bread crumbs and parsley. Spread the top of the meat with the mustard mixture, then press the coated side into the breadcrumb mixture.

Place the meat on a rack in a shallow roasting pan and roast for 25 to 30 minutes. Insert an instant-read thermometer into the thickest part of the lamb. It should register 135°F for medium rare. Remove from the oven and let rest for 5 to 10 minutes. Cut between the ribs to separate into chops.

Greek Lamb Stew

Many of Nick Forrest's Mediterranean, Middle Eastern and African customers in Oxford come to the Forrest Family Farm to buy lamb for holiday celebrations or religious observances; and many share their lamb preparations with the farmer, including this stew with a great Mediterranean flair.

Makes 6 servings

¼ cup all-purpose flour
Salt and freshly ground black pepper
3 pounds lamb shoulder, cut into 2-inch cubes
¼ cup extra-virgin olive oil
1 whole bay leaf
½ teaspoon ground thyme
1 teaspoon chopped fresh rosemary
1 clove garlic, crushed
2 cups lamb or chicken stock
1 cup white wine
1 (28-ounce) can tomato sauce
1 medium onion, coarsely chopped
½ cup black olives, pitted

Season the flour with salt and pepper. Dredge the lamb cubes in the flour mixture. Heat 2 tablespoons of the olive oil in a large Dutch oven over medium-high heat. In two batches, brown the lamb cubes in the oil, adding the remaining oil for the second batch. In the pot, mix the lamb cubes, bay leaf, thyme, rosemary, garlic, stock, wine, tomato sauce, and onion.

Cover and simmer over medium-low heat for about 1½ hours. Add the olives and simmer an additional 30 minutes. Remove the bay leaf, taste, and adjust the seasonings. Serve immediately or refrigerate overnight. Gently reheat before serving.

J & K JACOBS

John Jacobs
Hamler, Ohio

In September 1985, the spotlight was on Farm Aid and the struggle to save the small family farm. On the mall directly across from the dorm where John Jacobs lived while attending the University of Illinois at Champaign, Willie Nelson, Neil Young, and John Mellencamp tuned up for what was to become a concert of historic proportions, raising awareness and millions of dollars to help rescue struggling farms. It was a perfect atmosphere for this city boy from the suburbs of Chicago, who had spent his childhood on his grandparents' farm in Napoleon and was now working toward a degree in agriculture.

A few years later, John graduated and jumped straight from the campus into a career in farming, working for a large confined-hog operation in the south. It was factory farming at its worst. Animals spent their days in small metal crates in which they could barely move, lacking access to sunlight and fresh air. Heavy use of antibiotics and growth hormones, and a laundry list of problematic environmental practices stood in sharp contrast to the Farm Aid message, which asked that farmers work to ensure safe and healthful food for the people as well as protect the natural resources of the country. John quickly became disillusioned down this early path of his career, quit, and became an interstate trucker. Time on the road provided ample opportunity for thought—and his mind kept returning to farming.

John moved back to the northwest corner of Ohio, where his interest in farming was first sparked, and along with his father began J & K Jacobs, farming eighty acres of land growing corn, soybean and wheat. "I started out raising hogs like most farmers were in 1997," says John, when antibiotics used to reduce disease and promote growth were a standard part of the feed mix. Just as John was about to expand his hog production for the conventional market, that is, meat packaged under generic labels, prices for hogs plummeted, putting a new spin on his plans. "Hog farming isn't something you can walk in and out of when the market doesn't suite you," he says, "so you have to rethink the way you do things."

Encouraged by new trends in farming, John decided to scale down his herd to raise them in ways that were better for the animal, the land, and the customer. He started by allowing his hogs to "be themselves," to run, roam, and root in the fresh air. They were fed on healthy pasture and a high-fiber diet rich in his own farm-grown grains, without growth hormones or antibiotics.

Four hundred happy hogs leave J & K Jacobs farm each year, the majority of which are committed to Niman Ranch, a California-based ranch that works with about three hundred independent family farms all across the country. J & K Jacobs is the only Ohio hog farm producing for Niman Ranch. Notable chefs all across the country consider it prestigious to announce that fresh Niman Ranch beef, lamb, or pork is featured on their menus, a brand synonymous with flavor, health, and quality. Niman Ranch will only work with farms like J & K Jacobs, that raise livestock under a strict protocol, developed by the Animal Welfare Institute, which calls for humane treatment of the animals and environmental stewardship.

The way John raises his hogs requires more work and attention than the confinement system, his first introduction to hog farming, but it has its rewards and has earned him some well-deserved attention. His farming methods produce no odor and preserve the water supply, which makes him a good farming neighbor, sustaining the land and the community. "There's a bigger picture here than just raising pork," says John. "It's how I raise it, how I manage my farm, and what I leave behind for future generations." He knows that sometimes if you want something done right, you have to do it yourself. This thought may not have led him to farming, but it certainly makes him the farmer he is.

Ohio Pulled Pork with Vinegar and Onion Sauce

This recipe uses the pork shoulder, a prime cut that contains a higher level of fat than other cuts. The fat can easily be removed after cooking. The thin vinegar and onion dressing is a perfect counterpoint to the richness of the meat.

Makes 8 to 10 servings

Pulled Pork:

1 (5 to 6 pound) bone-in pork shoulder butt roast
½ tablespoon sweet or hot paprika
½ tablespoon coarse salt
½ tablespoon freshly ground black pepper
2 cups apple cider, water, or a combination of the two
1 fresh bay leaf
8 to 10 crusty rolls, split and lightly toasted

Vinegar and Onion Sauce

¾ cup cider vinegar
¼ cup water
2 tablespoons brown sugar
1 small onion, sliced thinly
1 clove garlic, minced
1 teaspoon salt
½ teaspoon freshly ground black pepper
Pinch of red pepper flakes, if desired

Preheat the oven to 350°F. Rub the meat all over with the paprika, salt, and pepper. Place in a deep roasting pan. Add the apple cider and bay leaf. Cover the pan tightly with foil and roast for 4 to 4½ hours, or until the meat shreds effortlessly with a fork. Remove from the oven and let cool slightly. When cool enough to handle, shred the roast, discarding any fat. Cover and keep warm.

Meanwhile, combine all of the sauce ingredients in a medium saucepan. Bring to a boil and let boil for one minute. Remove from the heat and let cool to room temperature.

Pour the sauce over the shredded pork and toss to distribute. When ready to serve, use tongs or a slotted spoon to mound the pork on a crusty bun. Drizzle a little of the dressing over the top, if desired. Serve immediately.

Garden Fresh Poppers

The meat from the side or belly of the pig becomes bacon when it is cured and smoked, and the abundance of fat gives it a sweet flavor and tender crispness. Wrapped around fresh stuffed jalapeños and grilled over the coals, the smoky goodness enhances the kick of the peppers.

Makes 4 servings

12 medium fresh red or green jalapeño peppers
4 ounces cream cheese, softened
1 teaspoon ground cumin (optional)
12 strips thick-sliced bacon
Toothpicks

Preheat the oven to 400°F or heat a grill to medium-hot. Cut the peppers in half lengthwise, leaving the stem intact. Remove the seeds and membranes, and stuff each half with about one tablespoon of cream cheese. Place the halves back together, wrap with a strip of bacon and secure with a toothpick.

Place the peppers on a baking sheet that has been treated with cooking spray. Bake for about 20 minutes, turning once, or until the bacon is crispy. Or cook on the grill until the bacon is crispy. Remove from the heat, let cool slightly, and serve.

Pork Chops with Sage Sauce

Pork chops are probably the least intimidating of all pork cuts because they are so easy to prepare. Recipes can be easily adapted to the different thickness of chops. Simply increase or decrease the cooking times. While this recipe is great for a heartier main course, it can be adapted for cutlets, too.

Makes 4 servings

2 tablespoons extra-virgin olive oil
4 boneless pork chops, ¾-inch thick
Salt and freshly ground black pepper
¼ cup balsamic vinegar
¼ cup chicken broth
2 tablespoons unsalted butter, diced and softened
1½ tablespoons chopped fresh sage
Fresh sage leaves, for garnish

Heat 1 tablespoon of olive oil in a large skillet over medium-high heat. Blot the surface of the pork chops dry with a paper towel. Sprinkle each chop with salt and pepper. In two batches, brown the chops, 5 to 6 minutes per side, adding the remaining tablespoon of oil for the second batch. Transfer to a warm platter and cover to keep warm.

Drain off any excess oil and return the skillet to the heat. Add the vinegar and chicken broth, stirring to loosen any browned bits from the bottom of the pan. Bring to a boil and reduce by half, 3 to 4 minutes, until thick and syrupy. Whisk in the butter. Stir in the chopped sage. Pour the sauce over the pork chops and garnish with fresh sage leaves.

Panfried Pork Medallions

The mild flavor of pork tenderloin makes it perfect for marinating or as a backdrop for flavorful sauces and spicy rubs. And with just a few cuts of the knife, it can be butterflied and stuffed, or cut into inch-thick steaks and pounded thin or, as in this recipe, cut into thin medallions, breaded and quickly panfried for a fast weeknight meal. A watchful eye will make sure the thin slices stay tender and juicy.

Makes 6 to 8 servings

2 cloves garlic, crushed
¼ cup grainy mustard
¼ teaspoon cayenne pepper
Salt and freshly ground black pepper
1 pound pork tenderloin, cut into ¼-inch medallions
2 cups coarse fresh bread crumbs
2 tablespoons grated Parmesan cheese
¼ cup flour
2 eggs, lightly beaten
Vegetable oil, for frying
Lemon wedges

Combine garlic, mustard, cayenne, salt and pepper. Brush a little bit of the mixture over each slice of pork.

Combine the bread crumbs and Parmesan cheese. Dip the pork slices in the flour, then in the beaten egg and then in the breadcrumb mixture to coat, shaking off the excess.

Place a large skillet over medium-high heat and add a ¼ inch of vegetable oil. When hot, fry the medallions in batches, taking care not to overcrowd the pan. Cook for 2 minutes on each side. Remove and drain on paper towels. Serve warm with lemon wedges.

ROSE RIDGE FARM

David and Deanna McMaken
Malvern, Ohio

In 1992, Dean Robertson, a fourth-generation beef farmer, gathered his family together to talk about his vision for their Malvern family farm. His weathered hands and work-weary body had made a long career and a modest living for his wife and five daughters out of plowing and planting the expansive pastures and tending the herds that grazed the steep ridge that rimmed his Carroll County farm, homesteaded two hundred years earlier by his Irish immigrant ancestors. As he looked around, he expressed his wish to see the land used as it always had been, as a working, productive farm—a family farm. For daughter Deanna, a newly retired elementary school music teacher, it was music to her ears, because that was her vision, too.

Deanna and her husband David, also a music teacher and high school band director, and himself raised on a dairy farm, had both just stepped away from thirty years in the classroom to "the only job paying less than teaching," quips Deanna. "But if this were just about money, we wouldn't be doing this." Their foray into farming was bolstered by the agricultural values instilled in them by their families: respect the land and the animals, know your customers, and provide them with a product you would be proud to put your name on. While some of the methods the McMakens use to farm and tend their herd differ from what her father may have used, they find that the wisdom of generations past is a sound model for their farming practices.

The McMakens raise about forty horned Hereford cows a year on a fraction of their 450-acre bucolic farm where, from most angles, you can see the fields of organically farmed grains, grasses, and corn that the couple grow exclusively for their herds diet. The old English breed was founded some two and a half centuries ago as a product of necessity. The lineage of the Herefords on Rose Ridge Farm can be traced back almost one hundred years. They are a good choice for these farmers who find that the breed's docile disposition and excellent maternal qualities make them easy to handle. Herefords also adapt easily to the land and midwest weather patterns and are highly efficient at converting native grasses to tasty and tender beef, the flavor of which some say rival that of the popular Angus breed. "We are not looking for the biggest the beefiest cows around," says Deanna, "rather we look for a balance in genetics. But the three most important characteristics we look for in our herd are health, health, and health!"

"We follow our own personal model for raising our cows, not a commercial model which takes them from birth to market weight quickly, usually under twenty-four months," says David. Deanna adds that, "We're pretty old-fashioned, taking our time and feeding them small amounts of corn, oats, spelt, barley, and rye for longer periods of time." The herd is also turned out to the grassy pasture and hills of the farm where the water is spring fed and there is plenty of healthy foliage for feasting including timothy, sweet clover, alfalfa, and brambles. The result is marbling as fine and thin as cobwebs throughout the meat, which contributes to the flavor and juiciness of each cut. "The taste reminds me of what beef used to taste like when I was growing up," says Deanna. The beef is then dry-aged a full twenty-one days to help develop flavor.

Soon after the McMakens took over the farm, Deanna discovered her great-grandfather's cash journal from 1899. At that time, a whole cow sold for just a couple hundred dollars, but what she was most impressed by is that the journal was filled with familiar names of friends and neighbors from in and around Malvern. "He was feeding his community," she remarks, and recognized that she and David were doing the same. "We know our network of customers by name and face because we sell to them at farmers markets," says Deanna. No middleman, just personal and friendly conversations between them and the people who eat the beef they raise.

"I want to know who's buying and eating our product and I want them to come back and tell me how they liked that steak or roast, how they prepared it, and how it tasted," says Deanna. "If they like it, they tell others so we can rely on our customers selling our meat for us."

On occasion, a customer will balk or challenge Deanna about the price of organically raised beef. She admits that she used to get defensive, perhaps even bristle, at the comment. "No one knows like I do what it takes to raise this quality of meat," she says. Deanna has learned that educating the customer about how they raise beef on Rose Ridge Farm is a better approach, and the question is now met with, "Let me tell you what we're trying to do."

Flank Steak with Fresh Herb Rub

One of the most flavorful cuts of beef is the flank. It's a lean, flat cut that's fairly tender, but if cooked too long and at too high a temperature, it can become tough. Best finished to rare, it takes about seven or eight minutes per side over a nice hot fire, plus a few extra minutes of resting time to reach perfection. One of the most important finishing steps is to cut the meat across the grain, for a nice, tender chew.

Makes 4 servings

1 (1½ to 2 pound) flank steak, lightly scored

Fresh Herb Rub:

¼ cup finely chopped fresh rosemary leaves
¼ cup finely chopped fresh parsley leaves
2 tablespoons finely chopped fresh oregano leaves
4 fresh sage leaves, finely chopped
4 cloves garlic, minced
1 tablespoon kosher salt
1 tablespoon cracked black pepper
½ cup extra-virgin olive oil

With a sharp knife, score the flank steak on both sides, making shallow diagonal slashes one inch apart in opposite directions, to create a diamond pattern. This will prevent the steak from curling up during cooking.

Combine the herbs, garlic, salt, pepper, and olive oil to make a thick paste. Rub on both sides of the steak. Let sit for 20 minutes at room temperature.

Prepare a grill to medium-hot. Cook the steak on each side for 7 minutes. Test for doneness by inserting an instant-read thermometer in the thickest part of the steak. It should read 125°F for rare or 130°F for medium. Remove from the grill, cover with foil, and let rest for 10 to 15 minutes. Cut the flank steak across the grain into thin slices and serve.

Garlic and Red Wine Pot Roast

Pot roast is one of those cold-weather dishes that fills the kitchen with earthy scents for an entire afternoon leading up to dinnertime. An economical dish, it's usually made with a cut too tough to be roasted, but when braised or simmered in liquid for several hours, becomes fall-off-the-bone tender.

Makes 4 to 6 servings

2 tablespoons vegetable oil
1 (4 to 5 pounds) pot roast (beef shoulder or boneless chuck)
2 carrots, peeled and diced
1 stalk celery with leaves, chopped
1 onion, chopped
2 heads garlic, separated, peeled and crushed
1 cup red wine
2 cups beef stock, divided
½ teaspoon salt
1 teaspoon whole black peppercorns, crushed
4 sprigs fresh thyme
1 fresh bay leaf
1 tablespoon cornstarch

Place a large Dutch oven over medium-high heat. Heat the oil, add the roast and sear the meat on all sides. Add the carrots, celery, onion, and crushed garlic. Reduce the heat to low, cover, and cook for 30 minutes. Add the wine, 1 cup of the stock and the salt, crushed pepper, thyme, and bay leaf. Cover and simmer over low heat for 2½ to 3 hours, or until the meat separates easily with a fork.

When done, remove the roast from the pot and keep warm. Strain the cooking liquid and vegetables into a bowl, pressing to extract the liquid. Return the liquid to the pot. Combine the remaining cup of beef broth with the cornstarch and add to the liquid. Bring to a boil, stirring constantly until thick and bubbly. Simmer for 10 minutes. Slice the roast across the grain into ½-inch slices and serve with the warm gravy.

Rosemary-Scented Beef Stew

Beef cows raised on farms like Rose Ridge Farm enjoy a much higher quality of life than do those confined to factory farms. Open pastures, the ability to move around freely, and carry out natural behaviors makes them less susceptible to illness, eliminating the need for the constant use of antibiotics. The extra attention comes through in the flavor.

Makes 6 servings

1½ tablespoons extra-virgin olive oil
1 medium onion, diced
2 cloves garlic, minced
1½ pounds cubed beef (stew meat)
4 cups beef stock
3 sprigs rosemary, tied into a bundle
5 medium potatoes, cut into 1-inch chunks
4 carrots, peeled and cut into 1-inch chunks
1 tablespoon cornstarch
Salt and freshly ground black pepper

Place a large Dutch oven or heavy-bottomed pot over medium-high heat. Heat the olive oil. Add the onion and sauté until soft and transparent, about 5 minutes. Add the garlic and sauté for an additional minute. Remove the onions and garlic with a slotted spoon and set aside.

Add the stew meat to the pot and brown on all sides, about 5 minutes. Add 3½ cups of the beef stock to cover the meat. Return the onion mixture to the pot with the sprigs of rosemary. Bring to a boil, cover, and reduce the heat to low. Simmer gently for about 1½ hours, or until the meat is tender.

Add the potatoes and carrots. Cover and cook for an additional 30 minutes, until soft. Mix the cornstarch with the remaining ½ cup of stock. Stir into the stew to thicken slightly. Add salt and black pepper to taste. Remove and discard the rosemary sprigs before serving.

Sirloin Steak with Garlic Butter

Once cuts like steaks or roasts are removed from the heat source, they will continue to cook as they sit and rest, adding up to ten degrees to the finished temperature. Most of the recipes you'll find for cooking pastured beef are created to achieve a rare to medium-rare finish. If you like your steak well-done, sear the meat quickly over a high heat on each side to seal in its natural juices and then reduce the heat to a medium or low setting until done.

Makes 4 servings

½ cup unsalted butter
4 cloves garlic, minced
2 teaspoons garlic powder
4 (8-ounce) sirloin strip steaks or rib eye steaks, about 1-inch thick
Salt and freshly ground black pepper
Extra-virgin olive oil, for brushing

Preheat the grill to medium-high. In a small saucepan, melt the butter over medium-low heat. Stir in the minced garlic and garlic powder. Set aside.

Pat the steaks dry with paper towels. Lightly brush both sides of each steak with olive oil and sprinkle liberally with salt and pepper. Place the steaks on the hot grill grate and grill for three minutes each side, with the grill cover down. Test for doneness by inserting an instant-read thermometer into the thickest part of the steak. It should register between 125°F for rare and 130°F for medium.

When the steaks are done, transfer to a warmed platter and brush the tops liberally with the garlic butter. Allow to rest for about 5 minutes before serving.

Red Wine and Balsamic Glazed Beef Tenderloin

The McMakens know that their customers' palates appreciate a little marbling throughout the meat, which they achieve by feeding their herd organically grown grains and corn in addition to plenty of pasture time. It's a particularly important feature in keeping cuts such as tenderloin and steaks tender during roasting or grilling.

Makes 8 to 10 servings

1 (5-pound) beef tenderloin, lightly trimmed of fat
Salt and freshly ground black pepper
2 tablespoons extra-virgin olive oil
¼ cup dry red wine, such as Cabernet Sauvignon
½ cup balsamic vinegar
4 tablespoons fresh chopped rosemary
4 sprigs fresh thyme, chopped
2 cloves garlic, crushed
Sprigs of fresh rosemary, for garnish

Pat the surface of the tenderloin dry with paper towels. Sprinkle with salt and pepper. Place in a shallow roasting pan or a resealable plastic bag. Combine the olive oil, wine, balsamic, herbs, and garlic, and coat the surface of the meat. Let marinate for at least 2 hours and up to 6 hours, turning occasionally.

Preheat the oven to 450°F. Place a large ovenproof skillet or heavy roasting pan over medium-high heat. Remove the meat from the marinade, pouring any of the remaining marinade in a saucepan. Bring the marinade to a boil and reduce until thick and syrupy, about 10 minutes. Remove the herbs and garlic.

Sear the meat in the skillet on all sides, 3 to 4 minutes a side. Transfer to the oven and roast for 25 to 30 minutes. Heavily baste the tenderloin with the marinade two or three times during roasting. Test for doneness by inserting an instant-read thermometer into the thickest part of the roast. It should register 125°F for rare or 130°F for medium.

Remove the roast from the oven and transfer to a cutting board. Cover with foil and allow to rest 10 to 15 minutes before slicing into ½-inch thick slices. Transfer to warmed dinner plates and serve, passing the marinade glaze.

SPECKLED HEN FARM

Brooke Hayes-Lyman
Cardington, Ohio

On a particularly cold February morning, Brooke Hayes-Lyman set out on a one-woman mission to save a dwindling heritage turkey breed. In her compact-size station wagon, she traveled from her Cardington farm, just north of Columbus, across Indiana and Illinois, through Wisconsin where the season's worst snowstorm slowed her trip to a crawl, and finally to Minnesota where a breeder waited with a trio of Narragansett, one hefty tom and two nervous hens, which they crated and loaded into her car. Feathers and endless gobbling filled the space and the open windows made for a frigid trip home that, in Brooke's heart, was worth thirty-six sleepless hours. When she put the turkeys into her barn, they instantly flew into the rafters where they lived for a few weeks until she could coax them down.

What might have struck some, including her own husband, as a little mid-winter insanity was actually the first step in Brooke's plan to restore authenticity and a sense of history to the table at Thanksgiving. "When people think of turkey, they typically think of the broad-breasted Market Whites," says Brooke. "It's merely the protein course at Thanksgiving, not the centerpiece, which it historically was for many years before the age of the 'industrial turkey.'"

Heritage turkeys were largely forgotten among consumers around the 1960s, when production farms began churning out large white-feathered breeds faster, often in three months, and much cheaper than small farms could raise heritage breeds. Out-of-sight and out-of-mind, the heritage breed populations dwindled dramatically, some like the Narragansett to near-extinction. In Brooke's opinion, the renewed interest in heritage breeds, even though limited to a small portion of the nation's 287 million turkey consumers, returns respectability to what is most surely America's most popular culinary tradition.

In early spring, Brooke takes a steady flow of orders from faithful customers, as well as a growing list of new ones, for heritage turkeys, the highlight of meals still months away. She dedicates a small portion of her yawning ten acres to raising turkeys on a pasture shared with chickens, a few ducks, a couple of geese, quail, a "watch goat" named Penny, and Senser, a long-legged hound. More than two hundred heritage turkeys representing four different breeds, each native to North America, define her flock. The Narragansett is the oldest heritage breed in the United States; and the Kardosh Bronze, a cross between a Narragansett and a wild turkey, is the model for every child's hand-drawn tribute to the turkey. In lesser numbers among the flock are Kentucky Bourbon Reds, heavy-breasted with richly flavored meat and a few handsome Blue Slates.

Firmly shunning the use of hormones and antibiotics to raise a bigger bird, Brooke opts for more time to raise a better bird. It takes twice as long, almost nine months, sometimes a full year, before she has raised a turkey fit for her customers. "Because they live longer than factory breeds, my birds build more muscle, and that means more flavor," says Brooke. "They will also have more subdermal fat, which they store for the upcoming winter. This is what will keep the meat moist when roasting, not saline basting injections." With a varied diet of wholesome grains, grass, homegrown sunflower seeds, insects, and apples that fall from the trees in the fall, her heritage breeds will develop more complex flavors over strictly grain-fed turkeys. The taste? "Different is the best description" she offers. "Because there is more dark meat, the flavor is stronger and sweeter and the texture is like that of a steak—smooth and a nice chew, not dry and chalky."

When it comes to farming, extra challenges, like preserving the lineage of a historical breed, excite Brooke, who also juggles a part-time nursing career and is mother to a young son, Aidan, her "right-hand." But it's the entire cycle of farming that feeds her passion. "I like to see things from start to finish and love how every day, every season, is different," she says. "I love the intensity of the spring and the beginning of the growing season and how crazy the summer becomes in the fields and pastures and selling at the markets. The fall is a busy time putting everything to bed and then winter rolls around and it's time to rest."

Turkey Brined in Buttermilk

To brine or not to brine? It comes down to a question of personal taste. Traditional brining is a process that enhances the flavor and increases the moisture content of lean meats using a salt, sugar, and water solution. A cultured buttermilk brine technique is equally as effective and a little more interesting. The cultures break down the proteins, tenderize the meat, giving the turkey a subtle tang as well as producing an extremely tender and juicy bird.

Brines one 15-pound turkey

1 turkey (about 15 pounds)
1 cup kosher salt
1 gallon cold buttermilk
½ cup brown sugar
4 cloves garlic, crushed
2 tablespoons whole peppercorns, crushed

Rinse the turkey inside and out, and pat it dry. Rub the salt all over the surface and in the cavity of the bird. Place the bird in a large, heavy-duty plastic bag or a large sturdy plastic container with a lid. Combine the buttermilk, brown sugar, garlic, and peppercorns, and add to the bag, sealing tightly. Place on a tray in the refrigerator, and brine, turning occasionally, for 24 hours.

When ready to roast, remove the turkey from the brine, rinse thoroughly, and pat dry. Discard the brine. Let the bird sit at room temperature for one hour before roasting.

Roasted Heritage Turkey

Naturally raised heritage turkey from Speckled Hen Farm won't yield the "mega" breasts of commercial turkeys, so there is a closer balance between dark and white meat. This actually makes it easier to roast the bird to perfection. Hot, quick roasting is a better technique than slow roasting and there's no need to truss the bird, which only pulls the legs closer to the body and makes them take longer to roast.

Makes 10 to 12 servings

1 heritage turkey (about 15 to 18 pounds)
¼ cup extra-virgin olive oil
¼ cup unsalted butter, softened
1 large onion, quartered
2 cloves garlic, peeled and crushed
1 fresh lemon, halved
1 apple, unpeeled, cored and quartered
1 bunch fresh parsley
6 sprigs fresh thyme
Salt and freshly ground black pepper

Preheat the oven to 450°F. Pat the surface of the bird dry with paper towels. Mix the olive oil and butter into a paste. Rub all over the surface of the turkey, under the breast skin, and into the cavity. Loosely stuff the cavity with the onion, garlic, lemon, apple, parsley, and thyme. Season the outside of the bird with the salt and pepper. Place on a roasting rack and roast for 30 minutes.

Drape a piece of oiled parchment paper over the breast. Reduce the oven temperature to 350°F and roast, basting frequently, until an instant-read thermometer inserted into the thickest portion of the thigh reaches 150°F. Total cooking time should be between 2½ and 3 hours. Remove from the oven, cover loosely with foil, and let rest for 15 minutes before carving.

Heritage Dressing

Stuffing is stuffing when it's inside a turkey. When it's prepared and baked on the side, it's dressing. Either way, there never seems to be enough to go around at the Thanksgiving table. This one features all the basics of a good dressing and lends itself to your own adaptation. Add chopped sautéed mushrooms, chopped apples or nuts, sausage, sage, rosemary, or whatever reflects the tradition at your table.

Makes 12 servings

12 cups cubed white bread
8 tablespoons unsalted butter
1 cup chopped onion
2 cups diced celery
½ cup freshly chopped parsley
Salt and freshly ground black pepper
2 eggs, lightly beaten
1 to 1½ cups turkey or chicken stock
½ tablespoon sweet paprika

Preheat the oven to 325°F. Spread the bread cubes on a baking sheet and place in the oven. Bake until the bread is dry and crunchy but not browned, about 8 to 10 minutes. Remove from the oven and let cool.

Melt the butter in a large skillet over medium heat. Add the onion and celery, and sauté until soft and translucent, 10 to 12 minutes.

Lightly butter a 9 x 13-inch pan. Place the dried bread cubes in a large bowl. Add the cooked vegetables and melted butter, parsley, salt, and pepper. Toss to combine. Add the eggs and stock, and toss until they are evenly distributed and the bread is moist. Spread in the prepared pan and sprinkle with the paprika. Bake for 1 hour, or until the surface is crisp and dry.

Cider-Braised Chicken

Brooke Hayes-Lyman named her Speckled Hen Farm for the Sussex breeds that roam the pastures. A wonderful dual-purpose bird, they are great meat chickens as well as layers, producing eggs with light brown shells. Brooke only sells chickens whole, leaving you the task of cutting it up once you get home. Use the breasts in this recipe but be sure to save the legs, thighs, and wings for other uses and the backs to use for chicken stock.

Makes 4 servings

2 tablespoons vegetable oil
4 boneless skinless chicken breasts, patted dry with a paper towel
Salt and freshly ground black pepper
¼ cup minced onion
½ cup apple cider
½ cup chicken stock
2 tablespoons Dijon or whole-grain mustard
Salt and freshly ground black pepper
2 tablespoons finely chopped parsley, for garnish

Heat the oil in a large skillet over medium-high heat. Season the chicken breasts with salt and pepper. Add to the pan and brown on both sides, about 3 minutes per side. Transfer to a plate and cover to keep warm.

Add the onion to the skillet and cook for about 1 minute. Add the cider and chicken stock, and cook over high heat until the liquid has reduced by half. Add the chicken to the pan, cover, and reduce the heat to low. Simmer for 5 minutes.

Remove the chicken breasts from the pan, place on a warmed serving platter, and cover to keep them warm. Raise the heat to high and reduce the cider sauce until ¼ cup remains. Stir in the mustard, and season the sauce to taste with salt and pepper. Pour the sauce over the chicken, garnish with the parsley, and serve hot.

Roasted Chicken

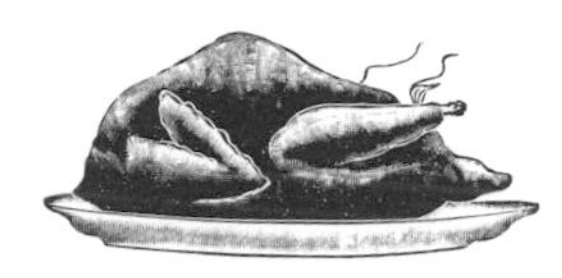

Few pleasures at the table can match that of a simply prepared, perfectly roasted chicken —crispy brown on the outside, moist and juicy on the inside. Allowing the bird to "rest" gives the juices a chance to equalize throughout the bird. The result? When the chicken is carved, you won't find puddles of juice on the cutting board—they remain inside the meat.

Makes 6 servings

2 tablespoons fresh lemon juice
1 clove garlic, minced
½ teaspoon coarse salt
½ teaspoon freshly ground black pepper
2 teaspoons dried oregano
¼ cup plus 1 tablespoon extra-virgin olive oil, divided
1 (3 to 4 pounds) chicken, trimmed of fat, rinsed, and patted dry with a paper towel

Preheat oven to 500°F. Combine the lemon juice, garlic, salt, pepper, and oregano. Stir in ¼ cup of the olive oil. Set aside.

Brush the chicken with the remaining tablespoon of oil. Place breast side down on a rack in a roasting pan. Roast for 20 minutes before turning breast side up.

Allow to roast for a few more minutes, or until the breast begins to brown. Baste with the lemon mixture. Reduce the heat to 350°F and roast for 30 to 35 minutes, basting two or three times, until an instant-read thermometer inserted into the thickest part of the thigh reads 160°F.

Pour the juices inside the bird into the roasting pan. Place the bird on a cutting surface, cover, and let rest for 10 minutes. Meanwhile, pour the pan juices into a small saucepan and bring to a boil over medium-high heat. Season to taste with salt and pepper. When ready to serve, carve the bird and serve with the pan juices.

Rich Chicken Stock

The difference between a good soup and one that's mediocre often lies in the stock. "Souper birds" will have less and tougher meat than roasting chickens but are perfect for creating the most flavorful broths and stocks, so rich that the broth seems almost creamy. Roasting the vegetables then gently simmering in the stock results in a rich, full-bodied taste that can be reduced to intensify the flavor for soups, stews, and sauces.

Makes 12 cups

3 carrots, scraped, trimmed and cut into 2-inch pieces
3 stalks celery, leaves attached, bottoms trimmed, cut into 2-inch pieces
2 onions, peeled and quartered
2 cloves garlic, peeled and crushed
1 large tomato, quartered
2 tablespoons extra-virgin olive oil
1 tablespoon whole peppercorns, lightly crushed
3 sprigs fresh thyme
2 fresh bay leaves
1 bunch fresh parsley
1 (3-pounds) chicken, cut up, or 3 pounds mixed chicken pieces (bones, wings, necks, or backs)

Preheat oven to 400°F.

Place the carrots, celery, onions, garlic, and tomato in a large bowl. Drizzle with the olive oil and toss to coat. Spread the vegetables on a baking sheet and roast for 25 to 30 minutes, or until lightly browned and fragrant. Remove from oven and place in a large stockpot, along with the peppercorns, thyme, bay leaves, and parsley. Place cut up chicken parts, including back, neck, and wings on top. Add cold water to just cover. Bring to a boil, and then reduce to a very gentle simmer. Skim off any foam that rises to the surface. Partially cover and cook for 3 to 3½ hours, or until the chicken falls from the bone.

Remove from the heat. Strain through a fine-mesh strainer lined with cheesecloth. Let the stock cool at room temperature for an hour, then cover, and place in the refrigerator for up to 48 hours. A layer of fat will congeal on the surface. Remove carefully with a spoon and discard.

The stock can now be used as a base in any soup recipe or frozen for up to 6 months.

FISH & SEAFOOD

TWENTY YEARS AGO, AQUACULTURE IN OHIO was limited to raising fish for bait and pond stocking. Surrounded by twelve river systems and flanking one of the nation's largest freshwater lakes, locally raised fish were the ones dangling from the end of your fishing pole, not harvested from a tank or pond.

In the early 1990s, the public's taste for freshwater fish began to exceed nature's supply, and prices for freshwater catches soared. Wild stocks in lakes and waterways were being seriously over fished, and troubling consumer advisories took the pleasure out of eating fish caught in local waters. It caught the attention of Ohio farmers, looking for another farming niche. They began to think outside the field, adding aquaculture tanks and ponds to their acreage, setting the pace for farming fish for food in Ohio.

Today aquaculture, which is defined as "the cultivation of the natural products of water," is one of the fastest-growing sectors of agriculture in the state. More than forty freshwater fish farmers harvest a continuous catch of yellow perch, trout, catfish, tilapia, and bass. In addition, there are more than thirty farmers pond-raising shrimp with great success and delicious results.

Freshwater Farms of Ohio

Polly's Prawns and Flower Farm

FRESHWATER FARMS OF OHIO

Dr. Dave Smith
Urbana, Ohio

Dr. Dave Smith is a marine biologist living in the driest part of the state. He's about one hundred miles from Lake Erie, the closest body of water, yet in his backyard are thousands of freshwater fish: rainbow trout, large-mouth bass, blue gill, yellow perch, channel catfish, even a school of sturgeon. Part of a growing number of farmers who are getting their hands wet as opposed to dirtied, Dr. Dave is one of the frontrunners in what he calls the "slow creep" of aquaculture into the state of Ohio.

Aquaculture, like agriculture, is indeed farming. There are seeds to be sown, in this case juvenile fingerlings in need of proper tending to grow to adult fish. The growing medium is water that, like soil, needs to be fertilized or nutritionally enhanced to produce a quality crop. And there is a harvest—a unique protein crop that requires a net, not a basket. The ultimate goal is that aquaculture, like agriculture, will provide a food source.

From the moment Dave caught his first fish as a child, he was quite literally hooked on aquatics and pursued his passion through leisure, hobby, and education. In the mid 1980s, while working on his PhD at the University of Wisconsin, he came across a story in a German aquatics magazine about raising freshwater fish in greenhouses. He knew the practice was deeply rooted in history. It traced back to ancient China, where the need to feed a lot of people called for innovation. Ohio's lakes and rivers are natural sources of fish but, to keep up with demand, commercial fisheries had a way of depleting the natural resources. Farm-raising fish was an environmentally friendly option that caught the newly degreed doctor's attention and one that he vigorously pursued upon his return to Ohio.

The long, narrow barn that stretches the length of Dr. Dave's Urbana farm served as a poultry barn in the 1940s. Dr. Dave replaced the coops with tanks, troughs, and a new purpose. Soon the barn echoed with the soothing sounds of circulating water and the occasional slap of a tail fin on the surface. Aquaculture, by simple definition, is the raising of aquatic organism in fresh, brackish, or salt water. Yet Dr. Dave is quick to point out that it's more than just a matter of putting fish in a tank and watching them grow. Instinctively foragers, fish need to be domesticated to get them to eat high-protein grain as their regular diet.

Solar panels keeps the barns cool in the summer and warm in the chilly Ohio winters, and maintain a constant temperature in the tanks to suit each species, from 59°F for rainbow trout to 70°F for yellow perch. Aerators run 24/7 to feed oxygen to the tanks, and a diesel-powered backup generator is the farm's watchdog. Dr. Dave doesn't worry much about natural predators, but a power outage creates panic like a fox in the henhouse, with the potential to eliminate an entire crop in a matter of hours.

All of the fish raised at Freshwater Farms are indigenous to Ohio, and under the controlled environment, Dr. Dave harvests all year round. Farm-raised fish also reach maturity quicker than the fish harvested in the wild, often in less than half the time. And just as the crop farmer can adjust the sweetness of the soil, Dr. Dave does the same with fish with adjustments to the pH of the water, and this contributes to a mild flavor.

A growing number of farmers in Ohio have integrated freshwater fish into their farming operations at the encouragement and instruction of Dr. Dave Smith. He puts a twist on the old maxim that if you teach a man to fish, he'll eat for a lifetime. If you show a man how to raise fish, he'll help feed everyone else, too.

Cornmeal Crusted Catfish

When it comes to freshwater-farmed fish, catfish are considered among the best for eating. The meat is lean, white, tender, and sweet and, when raised in clean waters, the flavor is mild and slightly nutty. Since it has little or no connective tissue, it does not have to be cooked long to be tender, which is the key to preserving the delicate flavor.

Makes 6 servings

6 (8-ounce) catfish filets
1 cup buttermilk
½ cup cornmeal
½ cup all-purpose flour
2 teaspoons ground cumin
Salt and freshly ground black pepper
¼ cup vegetable oil, plus extra if needed

Blot the catfish filets dry with a paper towel. Place the buttermilk in a shallow dish. Combine the cornmeal, flour, cumin, and salt and pepper in another shallow dish. Dip each of the filets into the buttermilk and then into the cornmeal mixture, coating each side evenly.

Place a large heavy skillet over medium-high heat. Heat the oil. When the oil is hot, add the filets, in two batches, if necessary. Fry for 4 minutes per side or until golden brown. Transfer from the skillet to a paper towel-lined plate. Serve with Sweet Pepper, Corn, and Bacon Relish (page 68).

Sweet Pepper, Corn, and Bacon Relish

Smoky bacon and fresh garden produce come together for a wonderful relish which can be used to accompany grilled pork chops or mild fish.

Makes 6 servings

3 slices bacon
1 green bell pepper, seeded and diced
1 red bell pepper, seeded and diced
1 small red onion, diced
2 teaspoons ground cumin
½ cup cooked corn
1 tablespoon fresh chives
½ teaspoon salt

Place a heavy skillet over medium-high heat. Place the bacon in the skillet and cook until some fat is rendered. Reduce the heat to low and cook until the bacon is crispy. Remove and drain on paper towels. When cooled, crumble the bacon.

Drain off all but ½ tablespoon of the fat. Return to the medium heat and add the peppers, onion, and cumin. Sauté until soft and fragrant. Add the corn and heat through. Remove from heat and add the chives, salt, and crumbled bacon. Serve warm or at room temperature.

Panfried Trout Cakes

Grown in the wild, rainbow trout can grow up to a hefty forty pounds. In contrast, farm-raised trout are one pound. It takes one year and one pound of food to bring them to market weight. Farm-raised trout has a wonderfully mild taste, firm texture, and few bones to tangle with, a perfect choice for these trout cakes.

Makes 4 servings

1¼ pounds trout filets, chopped coarsely
1 slice fresh white bread, chopped into crumbs
¼ cup finely chopped scallions
2 tablespoons chopped fresh parsley
2 tablespoons mayonnaise
1 teaspoon salt
1½ tablespoons freshly squeezed lemon juice
½ cup all-purpose flour
2 eggs
1 cup plain dry bread crumbs
Vegetable oil, for frying
1 fresh lemon, cut into 4 wedges

In a medium-size bowl, place the chopped trout, bread, scallions, parsley, mayonnaise, salt, and lemon juice. Mix well. Scoop ¼ cup of the mixture and form it into a patty about ¾ inch thick and 3-inches in diameter. Repeat with the remaining mixture. Place in the freezer for 30 minutes to firm up.

In one shallow dish, spread the flour; in a second, beat the eggs with a teaspoon each of vegetable oil and water; and put the bread crumbs in a third dish. Remove the trout patties from the freezer. Dip each patty on both sides into the flour, then the egg mixture, and then the bread crumbs.

Pour ¼ inch of the vegetable oil in a large heavy skillet and heat over medium-heat until hot but not smoking, about 3 minutes. Add half of the patties and cook for about 2 minutes on each side until golden brown and crispy. Remove to a paper towel-lined plate. Repeat with the remaining patties. Serve with lemon wedges and a dollop of Lemon Herb Sauce (page 70).

Lemon Herb Sauce

This versatile sauce can take on an entirely different personality by substituting fresh dill or snipped chives for the thyme. Serve it with your favorite fish or seafood.

Makes ¾ cup

½ cup mayonnaise
2½ tablespoons freshly squeezed lemon juice
1 tablespoon minced parsley
1 tablespoon minced fresh thyme
1 large scallion, minced
Dash of hot sauce
Salt and freshly ground black pepper

Mix all the ingredients for the sauce in a small bowl. Season to taste with salt and pepper. Let stand at room temperature for 30 minutes before serving. (Sauce can be refrigerated for up to 4 days.)

Beer-Battered Fish Fry

Yellow perch are the most popular food fish in the Great Lakes region. Although the majority are caught in the wild, farm-raised yellow perch are getting a lot of attention for their mild taste and health benefits that come with being raised in the fresh, clean waters of a farm environment. This beer batter creates a light, crispy coating for the thin, delicate filets. Serve this classic Friday night fish fry with hash browns and fresh coleslaw.

Makes 4 servings

1 cup all-purpose flour, for dredging
Salt and freshly ground black pepper
Oil for frying
2 pounds fish filets (perch, catfish, or trout), patted dry with paper towels

Batter:

1 cup all-purpose flour
1 teaspoon baking powder
½ teaspoon salt
1 egg
1 cup beer
1 teaspoon freshly ground black pepper
¼ cup vegetable oil

In a shallow dish, combine the dredging flour with salt and pepper.

Place all the batter ingredients in a large bowl and beat with an electric mixer until smooth.

Pour 2 to 3 inches of oil into a large skillet or Dutch oven. Heat over medium-high heat to 375°F.

Coat the filets in the flour, then dip into the batter. Fry in batches until golden brown, 3 to 4 minutes. Drain the cooked filets on paper towels.

POLLY'S PRAWNS AND FLOWER FARM

Polly Creech
Albany, Ohio

Polly Creech, a talented florist, harvests an acre and a half of big, beautiful flowers that she uses to create distinct arrangements, bridal bouquets, and wreaths. In late September, just about the time when the garden begins to fade and the blooms droop, Polly gears up for the biggest harvest of the season. The pond that sits behind her flowerbeds has spent the summer growing thousands of giant Malaysian river prawns, more commonly referred to as shrimp. It's not something one stumbles across on a regular basis in the hills of Appalachia, but that's the theme in this corner of the state: expect the unexpected.

A few years back, Polly read an article in the local newspaper written by the local county extension agent, Rory Lewandowski. He was about to launch a shrimp-growing research project to determine how well freshwater shrimp could be raised in southern Ohio, and he was looking for a few adventurous souls who had the land, and more important, the curiosity. Although the notion piqued Polly's interest, she was slow to take action. Flowers she could raise. Shrimp was a gamble. And then there was the issue with the pond—or lack of one—on her property.

Following a few conversations and meetings with the agent, the backhoes arrived and began digging the perfect haven for shrimp. The heavy clay soil that works against the notion of crop farming in Ohio's Appalachia was ideal for creating a watertight aquaculture pond. With the pond in place and an aerator working around the clock, Mother Nature filled the half-acre pond with water from melting snow and spring rains. Polly added organic and natural fertilizers, including soybean meal and alfalfa pellets, to create the "bloom" of plant growth, or plankton, that would become part of the diet for the growing shrimp.

Three weeks later, the stocking truck arrived, pumping juvenile shrimp into the pond—about eleven thousand total, give or take a few, because no one was really counting. Every evening for the next four months, Polly walked back to the pond to scatter a meal of high-protein feed across the surface of the pond. "It's not exactly like feeding chickens," she says. "Shrimp like to hang at the bottom of the pond, so I never see them." Every once in a while, Polly poured a ten-pound bag of sugar in the water, not for dessert but to help balance the pH levels in the pond, on which she kept a vigilant eye.

Throughout the summer, about 75 percent of the juveniles in Polly's pond matured to jumbo-size shrimp, about seven inches long, tip to tail. Some were cannibalized, and a few ended up in the beak of a blue heron or the claws of a raccoon but most survived.

On Polly's farm, the pond was dug on a higher elevation and fitted with an external drain at the base of a bank. When mid-October arrived, friends and volunteers gathered to watch and help as the "plug" was pulled and the pond drained of thousands of shrimp into waiting nets and an aerated holding tank. As the pond emptied, just like a bathtub might, the shrimp followed the flow of water into the nets. It's a pretty clean way to harvest, although a few dozen were left on the muddy bottom. Polly rolled up her pants, kicked off her shoes and made sure that the harvest was complete—no shrimp left behind.

Retail customers and a handful of chefs arrived on the day of the harvest to buy the fresh, jumbo-size shrimp by the pound. Half of the harvest was sold pond side and the rest were iced down and sold at the Athens Farmers' Market the next day. Any shrimp that remained were processed, frozen, and sold at different retail locations around the area. Then, the following spring, the pond was restocked with new juvenile shrimp.

Polly's first harvest was just short of 130 pounds—not enough to her liking or her bottom line. The following year, the harvest doubled, as it did the year after that. Next on her "to-do" list is to find a way to get the nutrition-rich pond water, that now runs off into a creek, to benefit the flowers in her garden. She'll have the winter to think about that, when the pond and her flowerbeds lay fallow.

Shrimp Stock

"My shrimp are sold live, heads, legs, and all," says Polly Creech. When she sells her catch at the Athens' Farmers' Market, she also spends time educating her customers about how to clean and ready the shrimp for cooking as well as the secondary benefits. "The heads, shells, and scraps make a wonderful stock for seafood soups and bisques," she says. "They are getting not just one meal but two."

Makes about 3 cups

3 tablespoons extra-virgin olive oil
1 small carrot, peeled and diced
1 stalk celery including leaves, diced
1 small onion, chopped
2 cloves garlic, chopped coarsely
1 teaspoon salt
3 to 4 cups raw shrimp shells and heads
6 sprigs fresh parsley, chopped
3 sprigs fresh thyme, chopped
5 to 6 cups water
Juice of ½ fresh lemon

Place a medium-size stockpot over medium-high heat. Heat the olive oil. Add the carrot, celery, onion, and garlic, and sauté until soft and fragrant, 8 to 10 minutes, sprinkling with the salt halfway through. Add the shrimp shells, parsley, thyme, and water. Bring to a boil, then reduce the heat and simmer until the liquid reduces by half. Remove from the heat and add the lemon juice. Using a fine-mesh strainer, strain out the vegetable scraps and shrimp shells. Refrigerate the stock for up to 3 days, or freeze for up to 3 months.

Shrimp Chowder

The secret between good and great chowder is time. Make the chowder and then give it a day or two to "age." The fabulous flavors of the vegetables, potatoes, and shrimp will mellow and meld into a hearty meal.

Makes 6 servings

4 tablespoons unsalted butter, divided
½ cup diced onion
2 cloves garlic, minced
½ cup diced green pepper
2 carrots, diced
2 stalks celery, diced
2 to 3 cups shrimp stock, plus extra to thin (see page 74)
½ cup all-purpose flour
1 cup diced potatoes
1 teaspoon dried thyme leaves
1 whole fresh bay leaf
2 tablespoons minced fresh parsley
1 cup half-and-half
1 pound fresh shrimp, peeled and cut into 1-inch pieces
Salt and freshly ground black pepper
Dash hot sauce

Place a large skillet over medium-high heat. Melt the butter and let it become slightly foamy. Add the onion, garlic, green pepper, carrots, and celery and sauté until soft, 10 to 15 minutes.

Place a stockpot over medium heat. Pour in the shrimp stock. Add the flour, and cook whisking constantly until thick and smooth. Add the sautéed vegetables, potatoes, thyme, bay leaf, parsley, and half-and-half. Reduce heat to low and cook, stirring occasionally, until the potatoes break easily when pressed with a spoon. Do not let the mixture boil.

Add the fresh shrimp. Heat through about 10 minutes, or until the shrimp are white and firm. Remove the bay leaf and season to taste with salt and pepper. Thin, if desired with shrimp stock or half-and-half.

Polly's Backyard Shrimp Boil

There's something wonderful and natural about celebrating a fall day with a backyard shrimp boil. Shrimp go straight from the boil to the bowl and into the waiting hands of guests willing to work for their supper by peeling away the shells. Sweet, moist shrimp are a treat alone or accompanied by a cocktail sauce.

Makes 6 to 8 servings

4 quarts of water
3 tablespoons paprika
4 sprigs fresh thyme
3 fresh bay leaves
1 large onion, chopped coarsely
4 cloves garlic, peeled and crushed
2 tablespoons mustard seeds
2 teaspoons dill seeds
1 tablespoon salt
1 teaspoon red pepper flakes
1 tablespoon mixed peppercorns, crushed
2 tablespoons cider vinegar
2 pounds fresh shrimp, heads removed

Place the water in a large stockpot. Bring to a boil over high heat. Mix in all the remaining ingredients except the shrimp. Return to a boil. Reduce the heat to low and simmer for about 30 minutes to blend the flavors.

When ready to cook the shrimp, bring the water back to a boil and add the shrimp. Let the water come to a boil again and then strain out the shrimp, which should be white and firm. Take care not to overcook. Serve with Cocktail Sauce (page 77).

Shrimp Cocktail Sauce

Some things just naturally belong together, like boiled shrimp and tangy cocktail sauce. Feel free to dial up the heat index with an extra shake or two of tabasco.

Makes about one cup

¾ cup chili sauce or ketchup
2 tablespoons prepared horseradish
¼ teaspoon sugar
½ teaspoon salt
½ teaspoon freshly ground black pepper
2 teaspoons fresh lemon juice
4 drops Tabasco, or more to taste
1 teaspoon Worcestershire sauce
2 cloves garlic, minced

Combine all the ingredients in a small bowl. Taste and adjust the seasoning, if necessary. Cover and refrigerate the sauce overnight to meld the flavors.

Shrimp and Shiitake Mushroom Angel Hair Pasta

One of the best suggestions Polly Creech offers for preparing her harvest of freshwater shrimp from her southern Ohio shrimp pond is to "keep it simple." Quick-cooking methods, such as grilling, sautéing, and baking, maintain the delicate texture of the shrimp, and the mild, sweet taste lends itself to all types of seasonings.

Makes 6 servings

2 tablespoons salt
1 pound angel hair pasta
½ cup unsalted butter
4 cloves garlic, minced
½ cup chopped fresh basil
2 pounds fresh raw shrimp, peeled
2 cups fresh shiitake mushrooms, sliced
1 teaspoon crushed red pepper flakes
½ cup chopped fresh parsley
Freshly grated Parmesan cheese, if desired

Bring a large pot of water to a boil. Add the salt. Add the pasta and cook for 6 to 8 minutes. Drain, reserving some of the water in a separate bowl. Cover to keep warm. Set aside.

Melt the butter in a large skillet over medium-high heat. Add the garlic and basil, and cook for 1 minute, stirring occasionally. Add the shrimp, mushrooms, and pepper flakes, and cook another 5 minutes, stirring occasionally, until the shrimp are no longer transparent, 4 to 5 minutes. Warm six dinner plates.

When ready to serve, pour a little of the reserved water over the pasta and toss to loosen. Divide the pasta among the six plates and top with the shrimp mixture. Sprinkle with chopped fresh parsley and grated Parmesan, if desired.

FRUITS & VEGETABLES

WOULD YOU TRAVEL 2,300 MILES across the country to bite into a vine-ripened tomato or a crisp apple? Probably not, but that's the trek many fruits and vegetables make to grocery stores. Rising produce prices are not a reflection of increased flavor or nutritional value, but rather in transportation costs.

Ohio fruit and vegetable farmers grow more than two hundred types of crops from apples to zucchini, in varieties from hybrids to heirlooms, field-grown to hydroponics. Some are organically certified and others naturally grown, but all are homegrown, harvested, traveling no farther than from the field to the roadside or a short distance to the local farmers' market.

To add interest and variety, nature sees to it that the selection changes constantly over the eight-month growing season, beginning with bundles of tender green asparagus, a sure sign of spring, and ending with bushels of speckled winter squashes and vivid orange pumpkins, that signal the growing season is coming to a close.

BEST of the Season
HEIRLOOM
TOMATOES

Oasis Acres

The Orchards of Bill and Vicky Thomas

Rich Gardens Organic Farm

Sage's Apples and Schultz Fruit Farm

Shafer's Produce

Sippel Family Farm

BRAMBLE CREEK FARM

Jackie LeBerth
Little Hocking, Ohio

For twelve years, Jackie LeBerth worked as a small-business consultant in Ohio's Appalachia region, where she helped a lot of people, particularly women, launch agriculture-related ventures. So powerful was their drive and purpose that Jackie would often walk away from their meetings feeling inspired and energized. "I felt like they were on to something I needed to be a part of," says Jackie. She saw these strong, determined women as survivors in a part of the state that, geographically and economically, has not always been kind to the farmer.

One day, Jackie reached an involuntary crossroad in her career. To the left, another desk job was waiting. To the right was her chance to find out what it was these women were doing that had captured her attention—and her heart. Without too much hesitation, Jackie and her husband, Mike Neely, purchased forty-six acres of land just a few miles from their 200-year-old home on the Ohio River, and attended what Jackie refers to as "berry-U," an intensive introduction to small-scale berry farming at the Ohio State University South Center at Piketon. Jackie and Mike set aside two acres to raise blackberries and raspberries for profit and without the use of chemicals. Some said it couldn't be done. "Watch us," they said.

Before the first shovel of dirt was removed from the land, Jackie and Mike created a business plan that said, "Don't go into debt, use what you have, refurbish the old, fix what needs fixing, and count on your friends." Donna "Grandma" Betts, a tough, wise, and neighborly Appalachian farmer with a charming "make do" attitude, quickly became Jackie's mentor and benefactor, giving the couple sixty bramble plants, which they planted on Thanksgiving Day 2001.

Jackie implemented a dual-phase pest management program. She calls phase one "bug hunting." "I know when and where certain pests show up," she says. "I catch them by hand, eliminating the problem." Phase two is an ornery rooster and a flock of heritage-breed "biddies" that live among the brambles in a moveable, protected chicken pen called the "chicken tractor." They provide three-season pest and weed control, and a reliable supply of fertilizer. "And if that isn't enough, they supply us with a steady supply of beautiful organic eggs," says Jackie. "It doesn't get any better than that."

Each year since the first planting, Jackie has added new varieties to the mix and Mike has perfected a trellising and gravity-fed irrigation system that supplies a reliable flow of water and nutrients to the flourishing brambles. More than three hundred quarts of berries are picked throughout the season and sold to a growing list of customers and area restaurants, or made into Bramble Creek jams or jellies.

The leap from the corporate office to the farm field is not always an easy one, and rarely is a farm the place where great fortunes are made, but according to Jackie, you can't beat the benefits package: a helping hand from a neighbor, getting another year's work out of a fifty-year old tractor by using balled twine, and quiet moments among the brambles with a deer and her newborn twin fawns as the audience.

Bramble Creek's Mixed Berry Gratin

Blackberries and raspberries, often called brambles, are close relatives of the strawberry. It's not at all unusual to find farmers like Jackie LeBerth, who grows all three. They have the same general requirements to flourish: well-drained soil and full sun. The perfect time to make this gratin is when all three fruits ripen simultaneously, a small window of opportunity at the end of June, but worth aiming for.

Makes 6 servings

4 to 5 cups mixed seasonal berries (hulled and quartered strawberries, and whole berries such as red raspberries and blackberries), washed
1 to 2 tablespoons granulated sugar
Pinch of salt
Zest from 1 lemon
4 slices bread, crusts removed
3 tablespoons unsalted butter, softened
¼ cup brown sugar
1½ teaspoons ground cinnamon
¼ teaspoon grated nutmeg

Preheat the oven to 400°F. Place the berries in a large bowl and toss with the sugar, salt, and lemon zest. Place in a lightly buttered gratin dish or 9-inch pie plate.

Tear the bread into pieces and place in the bowl of a food processor fitted with a steel blade. Process until the bread is coarsely chopped. Add the butter, brown sugar, cinnamon, and grated nutmeg and pulse until combined. Spread over the top of the berry mixture to form a crust.

Bake for 20 to 25 minutes, or until the crust is a golden brown. Remove from the oven and let cool before serving. Serve with lightly sweetened whipped cream or a scoop of vanilla ice cream.

Grilled Peaches with Berry Coulis

A coulis (pronounced "coo-lee") is a thin puree of fruit, most often made with sweet, ripe berries such as blackberries, raspberries, or strawberries, which tend to have tiny seeds that some might find unappealing. It's a little more work to remove them, but who would want to miss out on the fabulous flavors of the Ohio berry season. The puree is a wonderful complement to fresh broiled or grilled stone fruits or pancakes.

Makes 8 servings

4 cups fresh blackberries, raspberries, or strawberries
2 or 3 tablespoons honey
1 tablespoon lemon juice
4 whole freestone peaches, halved and pitted
¼ cup unsalted butter, melted
4 tablespoons brown sugar
½ teaspoon ground cinnamon

Place the berries, honey, and lemon juice in a blender or food processor and process until smooth. Let sit for 30 minutes before pressing through a strainer to remove the seeds. Set the coulis aside.

Preheat the grill to medium-high. Brush the cut sides of the peaches with the melted butter. Place on a cookie sheet. Mix the brown sugar with the cinnamon and sprinkle over the buttered surface. Place the peaches cut side down on the grill grate and grill until the brown sugar is melted and bubbly and grill marks appear on the fruit. Remove and let cool slightly.

Serve with a scoop of vanilla ice cream. Drizzle generously with the coulis.

Raspberry Tart in Nut Crust

Fresh raspberries naturally capture the spotlight in any recipe and pair naturally with this delicate, buttery nut crust. Because these little jewels of summer are so special, it's best not to complicate or overpower their flavor with too many ingredients. A little lime zest and ginger is all you need to enhance the incredible flavor.

Makes 8 servings

Crust:
1¼ cups all-purpose flour
¼ cup ground hazelnuts or almonds, toasted
½ teaspoon salt
2 tablespoons sugar
8 tablespoons chilled unsalted butter, diced
4 tablespoons ice water

Filling:
3 cups red raspberries, washed and dried
½ cup sugar
1 teaspoon peeled and grated fresh ginger
2 teaspoons lime zest
2 tablespoons cornstarch

To make the crust: Combine the flour, nuts, salt, and sugar. Rub or cut in the butter until the mixture resembles bread crumbs. Sprinkle the chilled water over the ingredients and mix until the dough comes together, adding more water if needed. Gather the dough into a ball and flatten it into a disk. Wrap in plastic wrap and chill for 40 minutes. Let stand for 10 minutes at room temperature before rolling.

To make the filling: Combine the berries, sugar, ginger, and lime zest and toss with the cornstarch.

To assemble: Preheat the oven to 400°F. Roll out the dough to about ¼-inch thickness. Press into a 9-inch tart pan with a removable bottom. Trim the edges. Spoon the filling into the shell and bake for 30 minutes until the crust is golden. Let cool completely before slicing.

Note: Black raspberries or blackberries may be substituted for the red raspberries in this recipe.

BRIDGMAN FARM

Mary Bridgman
Washington Court House, Ohio

When Mary Bridgman displays her heirloom tomatoes at the North Farmers' Market, in Columbus, shoppers gather around with curious looks. That's her cue to lead with a "beauty is only skin deep" lecture. She warns that on the outside, heirlooms aren't always the prettiest tomatoes in the bin. "They can be cat-faced, misshapen, or scarred," she cautions, "but it's what's on the inside that counts!"

Mary knows that sometimes all it takes to convert someone from the predictable taste of hybrids to heirloom tomatoes is the taste—rich, full, aromatic, and, in the same bite, both sweet and tangy. Offer people a taste of Sugar Lump, German Red Strawberry, or Black Krim tomatoes, and they'll find it hard to resist. If the taste doesn't reel them in, there are stories behind many heirlooms that tell of their travels or a special place in history. In the late 1800s, the Polish tomato, a thick brick-red globe, was brought to Ohio by immigrants who smuggled the seeds in on the back of a postage stamp. Mortgage Lifter tomato, a prolific grower with big, meaty pink-red fruits, was grown and sold by a farmer facing bankruptcy in the 1930s to help pay off his mortgage.

Raising heirloom tomatoes is a full-time passion for this lady farmer, a retired writer and photographer for the *Columbus Dispatch*. At last count, she tends over fifty-two varieties of tomatoes on her sixty-seven-acre organic farm in New Washington Court House, which she sells at farmers' markets and to Columbus-area restaurants. That's three thousand plants, most of which are heirloom varieties, with a few hybrids thrown in for the sake of familiarity.

By strict definition, an heirloom is a valued possession that has been handed down from generation to generation. By working definition, for any fruit or vegetable to be considered an heirloom, the variety must be at least two generations old, and must be open-pollinated, which means that nature, not man, takes care of the process. By this means, the desirable and unique characteristics of the tomato, including taste, texture, color, amount of seeds, and sweetness or acidity are kept pure for the enjoyment of generations to follow.

"Heirlooms aren't the easiest vegetables to grow, nor the easiest to sell," admits Mary. "They are not bred for all the things Mother Nature can throw at them, but it's still worth it." Good garden hygiene practices are a must to stave off disease and pests, and even then, a portion of the crop will fall victim. The Brandywine tomato, perhaps most responsible for the resurgence in heirloom tomatoes because of its superb flavor, cracks easily and ends up in the compost pile as often as at the market. Mary blankets her tomato rows in black plastic to cut down on weeds, warm the soil, and grow smaller tomatoes, which have more flavor. Add a drought or a year with below average rainfall, and the tomatoes will have a more intense flavor and a meatier texture and will be less likely to swell and split their thin skins. "When cherry tomatoes end up being the size of a penny, they are just bursting with flavor," she says.

Like snowflakes, the tomatoes in Mary Bridgman's fields are wildly different from one variety to the next. There's a wide range of shapes and colors, from the pale skins of the Caspian Pink tomato to the fiery-red Druzba tomato. The dusky brown tones of the tomato called Black from Tula always get a second look, as do Aunt Ruby's German Green Tomato and the spectacular Big Rainbow tomato's resplendent splashes of reds and yellows. Goldie has a bright yellow neon glow, which is a great contrast to the White Wonder tomato or the grassy shade of the Green Zebra. Their shapes can be equally unconventional—deeply pleated such as the Pineapple tomato, elongated such as the Speckled Roman, ox-heart shaped like the Anna Russian, or the petite teardrop contour of the Yellow Pear cherry tomatoes.

When the days in the tomato-growing season begin to wind down, Mary finds herself working harder to turn people on to the taste of heirloom tomatoes. She takes great pride in her power to make her customers dread the first frost. "When that comes around, homegrown tomatoes are gone for nine months," she says. "That's a long time to wait for another great-tasting tomato."

Heirloom Tomato Gratin

This recipe depends on the taste of the tomatoes, so Mary Bridgman suggests sticking to one variety for the most impact in flavor. Black and purple tomatoes have deep, smoky flavors, while bicolor tomatoes such as the Big Rainbow can be very sweet. Mary's hands-down favorite choices would be Brandywine or Goldie, but if you want to make a statement with color, be sure to seek out German Strawberry.

Makes 8 servings

Gratin Mixture:

3 slices soft white bread, torn into pieces
1 tablespoon extra-virgin olive oil
2 teaspoons grated lemon zest
1 clove garlic, minced

Filling:

2 tablespoons extra-virgin olive oil, plus extra
1 tablespoon unsalted butter
1 large sweet onion, sliced thinly
6 large, meaty tomatoes, cut into ½-inch slices and then cut in half
2 tablespoons fresh chopped thyme
Salt and freshly ground black pepper
½ cup freshly grated Parmesan cheese

Preheat oven to 400°F.

To prepare the gratin mixture, place the torn bread, oil, lemon zest, and garlic in a food processor and process into fine crumbs. Set aside.

Heat the olive oil and butter in a large skillet until the butter is melted. Add the onion and sauté on high heat for about 5 minutes. Reduce the heat to medium-low and continue to cook until the onions are soft and brown, 15 to 20 minutes. Remove from the heat and set aside.

Brush a heavy gratin dish or a rectangular baking dish with oil, and dust with a couple tablespoons of the gratin mixture. Spread the caramelized onions on the bottom. Tightly layer the tomato slices in the baking dish. Sprinkle with chopped thyme, salt, pepper, and cheese. Spread the remaining gratin mixture on the top and drizzle with a little olive oil.

Bake uncovered, for 35 to 40 minutes or until the tomatoes are soft and the bread crumbs are golden and toasty.

Heirloom Tomato Salad

Mary Bridgman recalls a shopper who looked curiously at a pile of large, fruity Brandywines, her best-selling heirloom tomato. "He didn't like their cat-faces, which is typical of the variety." Ultimately he walked away, missing out on the incredibly rich flavor. The variety is eighty years old, preserved for future generations by Ben Quisenberry, an Ohio gardener. You'll find them in colors ranging from pale pinks to flaming reds to mix up in this simple salad.

Makes 8 servings

4 red, yellow, or pink Brandywine tomatoes, cut into ¼-inch slices
1 pound fresh mozzarella cheese, cut into ¼-inch slices
12 large fresh basil leaves
Extra-virgin olive oil
Balsamic vinegar, preferably white balsamic
Freshly cracked black pepper
Coarse sea salt

Lay the sliced tomatoes overlapping in rows on a platter, alternating with the mozzarella slices.

Cut the basil leaves into 'ribbons' by stacking six leaves and rolling up tightly like a cigar. Using a sharp knife, cut thin strips from the tip of the leaf to the stem end. Fluff to separate. Repeat with the remaining leaves. Sprinkle on top of the tomatoes.

When ready to serve, drizzle the tomatoes and mozzarella with a little olive oil and a splash of balsamic vinegar and season to taste with salt and freshly ground black pepper.

Tomato Bruschetta

From her stand at the North Farmers Market or the Clintonville Farmers Market, Mary Bridgman educates customers about how to choose the perfect tomato. "Does it smell like a tomato?" she asks. "Good tomatoes have a sweet, fruity fragrance." This recipe relies on garden-ripe Romas such as Sausage or Mama Rosa's, a bright orange, thick-fleshed tomato.

Makes 8 to 10 appetizer servings

2 cloves garlic, peeled and minced
8 large Roma or plum tomatoes, cored and coarsely chopped
2 tablespoons freshly chopped basil
2 teaspoons extra-virgin olive oil, plus extra for brushing
Splash of red wine vinegar
Salt and freshly ground black pepper
2 10-inch baguettes, cut into ¼-inch slices

To prepare the tomato salad: In a medium bowl, combine the garlic, tomatoes, basil, oil, and vinegar. Season to taste with salt and pepper. Stir until blended. Refrigerate if using the next day or serve at room temperature.

To prepare the baguettes: Preheat the oven to 375°F. Brush the tops of the bread slices lightly with olive oil. Arrange on a baking sheet and place on the middle rack of the oven. Bake for 10 to 12 minutes, or until golden brown. Remove and let cool. (The bread may be stored in an airtight container until needed.)

To serve, top the bread slices with about a tablespoon of the tomato mixture.

Oven-Dried Cherry Tomatoes

Nothing comes on with a vengeance in the summer like cherry tomatoes. Drying them in the oven turns them into something new at the table. Look for Matt's Wild Cherry, a sweet tasting, prolific grower; Snow White, pretty, pale, and mild in taste; or Juliettes, flavorful fruits that look like miniature Romas. Mix varieties for a dynamic range of tastes, from sweet and mild to acidic and wild. Add to pasta and vegetable dishes, on top of pizza or in a salad.

Makes 8 servings

2 to 3 pints cherry tomatoes, cut in half horizontally
Extra-virgin olive oil
Kosher salt
Freshly ground black pepper

Preheat the oven to 200°F. Line a large baking sheet with aluminum foil. Place the tomatoes cut side up on the baking sheet, drizzle lightly with olive oil and sprinkle liberally with salt and pepper. Bake in the center of the oven for 2 to 3 hours or until the tomatoes have shrunk to about three-fourths of their original size. Serve hot, at room temperature, cold, or allow to cool and store in an airtight container in the refrigerator for up to 8 weeks.

JUST THIS FARM

Kevin Eigel
Galion, Ohio

When Kevin Eigel lived and worked as an English teacher in Japan, he would go to the local *izakaya,* a Japanese-style tavern, at the end of his workday to refresh himself, chatting with friends and co-workers and enjoying a beer or a sake, which almost always arrived with a bowl of steamed and salted edamame (pronounced "eh-da-mah-may"). For a boy who grew up in Ohio, soybeans were not snacked on like peanuts or pretzels. They were an agricultural commodity that defined Ohio's landscape—acres upon acres of leafy plants left to dry into tough, brown seeds, then harvested in great quantities to be shipped and processed into diesel oil, pesticides, or salad dressings.

Kevin spent three years in Japan, where he grew to love the culture, people, traditions, and food. So when he returned to Ohio and decided to farm, growing the foods he enjoyed overseas was a natural direction, and edamame an easy choice. Edamame, which means "branch bean," are the same species as the familiar soybean and have been a part of the Asian diet for thousands of years, but only in the last ten years have American cooks taken notice. In Ohio, where more than four million acres of soybeans are grown, edamame is creating a buzz among gourmets who have discovered the tender bean with the smooth texture and nutty flavor. "The difference between edamame and the soybeans you see in the fields is like the difference between sweet corn and field corn," says Kevin. "One has taste and texture, and the other has none."

Kevin's thirty-five-acre farm, called Just This Farm, is an extension of his practice of Zen Buddhism. "It's all about paying attention to the present," says Kevin. "Just this moment, just this place, just this farm." It sits east of the central Ohio Darby Creek Watershed, which has been designated by the Nature Conservancy as "The Last Great Place," and distinguished by the Ohio Environmental Protection Agency as an exceptional warm-water habitat and site of outstanding state water. It's a great complement to his organic farming practices. Cows, sheep, and chicken pasture fifteen acres, and another three acres grow an eclectic variety of Asian vegetables, such as Japanese sweet potato and white turnips, daikon radishes, Chinese green cabbage, kabocha squash, garlic, and greens. Only a small fraction of Kevin's crop is the gourmet soybean. "It's labor intensive, hard to grow and harvest," he says, "but everyone likes to eat it, including rabbits, ducks, and deer."

When bunched together, the spindly green stalks dangle coarse fuzzy pods about two inches long, each holding two or three beans. They always get a second look from shoppers who curiously take the steamed samples and squeeze the contents from the pod into their mouths. Although most of Kevin's sales are to Asian customers, the locals are catching on, reeled in by the flavor and the nutritional benefits of this protein-rich legume high in calcium, iron, and zinc.

"Ideal weather, good soil, and water are necessary for farming, but that's not what keeps my farm growing," he says. "It's people who want to eat well and are looking for good, wholesome healthy foods—that's what keeps it growing."

Steamed Edamame

Like corn, edamame is best enjoyed freshly harvested and simply prepared—cooked quickly and salted. The pods are not edible, only the beans. Steamed and shelled, they can also be tossed into stir-fries, mixed with mashed potatoes, and added to soups, salads, and chilis.

Makes 6 appetizer servings

6 cups water
1 tablespoon salt
1 pound fresh edamame
Coarse salt to season

Place the water and tablespoon of salt in a large pot and bring to a boil over high heat. Add the edamame beans to the water and cook for 5 minutes. Drain and let the beans cool for 30 minutes. Season with coarse salt.

To eat, raise the salted pods to your mouth and squeeze the beans into your mouth. Discard the pods. Serve with a glass of beer or sake.

Spicy Edamame Dip

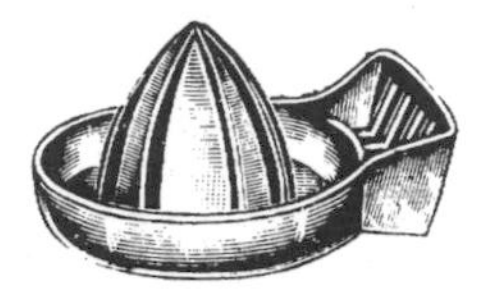

In Japan, edamame was traditionally used as a summer food to be enjoyed with the viewing of the full moon in September and October, a lovely thought if you are able to wait. Fresh edamame is admittedly hard to find, even in the biggest farmers' markets, but is well-worth the search. Many specialty grocery stores carry both organic and non-organic varieties in their freezer section year round.

Makes 12 appetizer servings

4 large garlic cloves, unpeeled
¼ cup extra-virgin olive oil, plus extra for brushing
2 cups shelled edamame beans
1 teaspoon salt
½ teaspoon ground coriander
½ teaspoon ground cayenne pepper
¼ teaspoon ground cumin
¼ cup freshly squeezed lime juice
¼ cup chopped fresh cilantro
Toasted pita wedges

Brush the garlic cloves with olive oil and place in a small skillet over medium-high heat. Cook, turning frequently, for 3 minutes. Then reduce heat to low and continue cooking until the cloves have softened, about 10 minutes. Remove from the heat and set aside to cool.

Bring a large pot of salted water to a boil. Place the edamame beans in the water and cook for 5 minutes. Drain, reserving 1 cup of the cooking liquid. Set aside to cool.

Squeeze the garlic out of the peel into the bowl of a food processor fitted with a metal blade. Add the cooled edamame beans, salt, and spices. Process, adding some of the reserved cooking liquid, until the beans are the consistency of peanut butter. Add the ¼ cup of oil, lime juice, and cilantro, pulsing to combine. Serve at room temperature with toasted pita wedges.

Corn, Edamame, and Red Onion Salad

Kevin Eigel has been raising edamame on Just This Farm not only for the taste and health benefits—they improve his soil, are easy to sell, profitable, "and I enjoy eating them," he says.

Makes 6 servings

2 tablespoons white balsamic vinegar
2 tablespoons cider vinegar
1 tablespoon brown sugar
½ teaspoon ground cumin
½ teaspoon onion powder
1 clove garlic, crushed
1½ cups shelled edamame beans
1½ cups cooked fresh corn kernels
½ cup red onion, diced
½ teaspoon salt
½ cup chopped fresh cilantro

Place the vinegars, sugar, cumin, onion powder, and crushed garlic in a small saucepan and heat until the sugar is dissolved. Remove from the heat and set aside to cool.

Bring a large pot of salted water to a boil. Place the edamame beans in the water and cook uncovered for about 5 minutes. Drain and let cool for 30 minutes.

In a separate bowl, combine the cooked edamame, corn, red onion, and salt. Remove the garlic from the dressing. Pour the cooled vinegar dressing over the mixture and stir to combine. Let sit at room temperature for 1 hour before serving. Stir in the cilantro just before serving.

MULBERRY CREEK HERB FARM

Mark and Karen Langan
Huron, Ohio

Mark Langan often feels more like a teacher than an herb farmer. Even the sales catalog that he and his wife and partner, Karen, publish is an informative read, more like a valuable reference book than a sales tool. Mark's goal is like that of any good teacher: get your students enthused about the subject, leave them wanting more, and always present them with new challenges.

During the sales season, visitors to Mulberry Creek Herb Farm, a two-acre organic herb farm in Erie County, will ask the same three questions of Mark and Karen: "How do I grow mint without it overtaking the garden?" "How can I grow a continuous crop of cilantro?" and the most frequently asked question, "How can I winter a rosemary bush?" Simple questions for the knowledgeable farmers, and between the two, they've recited the answers hundreds of times: "Grow mint in a pot to keep its vigorous roots contained; cilantro is a self-sowing weed, so let some of it go to seed for a continuous harvest; and rosemary plants like to drink in the cold, so put them in a sunny but drafty spot in the house."

You would think that the repetitive questions would wear on the herb farmers, but Mark and Karen consider them valuable clues in identifying novice herb gardeners, fresh students, and eager learners in search of some tutoring. The Langans know that the hungriest of students are enticed by looking at the most common herbs in a new light.

Parsley, an accessory to the plate that often doesn't get the attention it deserves is the perfect example. "Did you know that parsley is a culinary Band-Aid?" offers Mark. "When you go overboard on the garlic in the pasta sauce, add a handful of parsley to counter the harshness. It can temper too much of a good thing."

One of Mark's favorite points to ponder is the bay leaf, tops in the hierarchy of aromatic herbs but often glossed over, left to dry and go brown in the kitchen cupboard. "Once picked, the bay leaf loses 50 percent of its flavor within six months," explains Mark. "After sitting around a year, it has zero flavor benefits. The true flavor is sweet when it's fresh but bitter when it's dried." Mark gets customers to think outside the grocery store and plant a bay laurel in the garden, which can then be dug up, repotted, and wintered inside, extending its benefits to soups and stews over the winter months.

Once the basics are mastered, Mark introduces his customers to rare and unusual herbs, such as the root beer plant, a big leafy herb with fragrant, sweet, edible leaves used as a wrapper for fish, pork, and tamales; or Cuban oregano, with dime-size fleshy leaves, an unexpected crunch, and a taste that straddles mint and classic oregano. Mark saves his biggest lecture for last—the one on the sense and benefits of farming organically. Mark and Karen farm this way because they live and play here along with their young sons, Ben and Joshua.

"If you look at the history of pesticides, fertilizers, and fungicides, you'll see that most of these chemicals appeared after World War II," says Mark. "Before that, farmers used basic common sense methods of farming." He uses the same methods throughout his herb fields and greenhouse including organic composting and diversified plantings, which essentially incorporates a variety of plantings in close proximity, a practice that in Mark's experience, "confuses the heck out of the pests."

Every season there's something new for the herb-farming couple to learn along with the opportunity to share it with their customers. One year, it will be how to get lavender to survive multiple seasons ("Let the leaves blanket it in the fall, and when spring rolls around, cut the plants back to two-inch stumps."); the next, it will be turning the adventurous onto chocolate-covered garlic. Its all part of Mark's value-added lesson plan. "With every purchase, you get a lecture," he says—and maybe a little homework, too.

Bay Laurel Peaches

Karen Langan's profession and passion has yielded some of the most unique uses for every herb, especially bay leaf, perhaps the most overlooked and neglected herb in the cupboard. In recipes that call for "sweet bay" or "bay laurel," it's important to use a very fresh leaf and add it early in the cooking process as it takes time and heat for the leaf to give up its flavor and permeate the food.

Makes 8 servings

4 fresh peaches, halved and pitted
½ cup sweet white wine, such as Riesling
1 fresh bay leaf
2 tablespoons honey
1 teaspoon vanilla extract
2 tablespoons unsalted butter, cut into small dice and at room temperature
8 slices of vanilla pound cake, or 8 scoops of vanilla ice cream

Preheat the oven to 325°F. Arrange peaches cut side up in an 8-inch square baking dish. Set aside.

In a small saucepan, combine the wine and bay leaf. Bring to a boil and cook for 5 to 7 minutes, or until reduced by half. Stir in the honey and vanilla until blended. Whisk in the butter until smooth. Pour over the peaches. Bake, uncovered, for 20 to 25 minutes, or until the peaches are thoroughly heated and soft, but still holding their shape. Remove the bay leaf before serving. Serve the warm peaches over pound cake or vanilla ice cream. Drizzle with the remaining syrup.

Corn Tamales Wrapped in Root Beer Leaves

The root beer leaf, also known as Mexican pepper leaf, is not the source for a root beer float but it does have a similar fragrance and a sweet taste often compared to anise and cloves. This eight-inch heart-shaped leaf is frequently used in Mexican and Indian cooking as a flavor component, and as an edible wrapper for meat fillings as well as for corn tamales.

Makes 16 tamales

5 cups freshly cut corn kernels
⅓ cup milk
2 tablespoons sugar
½ teaspoon salt
2 tablespoons unsalted butter, softened
16 root beer leaves, 6 to 8-inches in diameter, plus extra to line the steamer basket (see note)

In two batches, process the corn in a food processor at a high speed, adding half the milk to each batch in a thin stream. Do not puree. Mixture should look coarse and somewhat lumpy. Transfer both batches to a large bowl. Stir in the sugar and salt, and mix well. Add the softened butter and mix until thoroughly combined.

Spread a leaf on a flat surface. Place a tablespoon of filling in the center and roll up cigar-style, folding the ends under so the long seam is facing upward. Repeat with the remaining filling and leaves.

Place a steamer basket in the bottom of a large pot filled with water to just below the bottom of the basket. Line the basket with a few leaves and stack the rolled leaves in a few layers, seam side up. Place the pot over medium-high heat. When the water comes to a boil, reduce the heat to a simmer, cover, and steam for 1 hour. Once cooked, let the tamales cool, uncovered, for at least 20 minutes so the leaves remain moist, not wet. Serve with salsa or sour cream.

Note: If root beer leaves are not available, substitute dried cornhusks that have been soaked in warm water for an hour to soften. Drain and shake off excess water before filling.

Minted Melon Salad

With almost a thousand different varieties of mint on record, Karen Langan takes care to choose wisely before adding just any mint to a recipe. "To flavor a beverage or fruit salad, I'll use orange, pineapple, apple, or Kentucky Colonel spearmint. I reserve strongly scented peppermint and chocolate mint varieties for swirling in coffee." Note that the strawberry vinegar for this recipe should be prepared three weeks in advance.

Makes 6 servings

Melon Salad:

2 cups watermelon balls
2 cups cantaloupe balls
2 cups honeydew balls
¼ cup chopped fresh mint leaves, plus extra sprigs for garnish

Dressing:

½ cup chopped and seeded watermelon
¼ cup fresh strawberries or raspberries
1 tablespoon Ohio honey, or more to taste
2 teaspoons raspberry or strawberry vinegar, or other fruit-flavored vinegar (page 103)

In a large bowl, combine the melon balls and chopped mint leaves. Toss gently and refrigerate until needed.

To prepare the dressing, purée the watermelon, strawberries, honey, and vinegar together in a blender or food processor. Taste and adjust for sweetness by adding more honey. Just before serving, toss with the melons and garnish with a sprig of mint. This salad is best served chilled.

Strawberry Vinegar

Fruit vinegars add a special freshness to any vinaigrette and are so simple to create. Seize the season by substituting blueberries, raspberries, black raspberries, black berries, or peaches for the strawberries.

Makes about 3 cups

2 cups cider vinegar
1 cup sliced strawberries
1 to 2 tablespoons honey
3 sprigs fresh thyme
A few small whole or sliced strawberries

Place the vinegar and sliced strawberries in a non-reactive saucepan and warm gently over low heat. Do not boil. Remove from heat and stir in the honey. Set aside to cool. Meanwhile insert the sprigs of thyme and berries in a 16-ounce sterilized glass bottle fitted with a cork. When the vinegar is cool, transfer to the bottle, cork and let sit for about three weeks to allow flavors to meld.

OASIS ACRES

Glen and Lois Smucker
Orrville, Ohio

With a name like Smucker, you have to be from Ohio. The jam and jelly giant proudly put Orrville on the map. Open the local phone book and you'll find about three inches of Smuckers, all descendents of the Ohio Amish and Mennonite settlers dating back to the 1800s. Only a small fraction have a direct connection to the worldwide brand.

That's true of Glen and Lois Smucker, who share a 175-acre family farm with Glen's father, 96-year-old Merl, a former dairy and grain farmer who has lived in the main house on this land his entire life. From the Smuckers' kitchen window is one of the best views of the prime Ohio farmland, rolling fields of corn and soybean and green grazing pastures. But in their backyard, a crop of lush salad greens and herbs is grown and harvested year round without a speck of the fertile, glaciated soil that characterizes Wayne County.

The Smuckers call their hydroponic greenhouse Oasis Acres. In terms of size, it is probably no bigger than a large backyard in the suburbs, but in terms of yield it is the equivalent of about twenty-three acres. Year round, the couple nurses a variety of greens and herbs, from delicate seedlings to full, lush, and leafy heads ready to make the routine Saturday morning trip to farmers' markets and restaurants in a four-county area.

At any one time, ten thousand plants in various stages of growth thrive in a "soilless" or hydroponic culture. Seeds germinate and grow in a substrate or growing material called spun rock wool, compressed strands that hold water, air, and the thirsty roots. Throughout the bright and airy greenhouse, row upon row of waist-high, narrow, shallow troughs circulate the constant flow of nutrient-enriched water to the neatly spaced plants. It takes about six to seven weeks to grow marketable greens under these conditions, two weeks less than in the field. As best as Lois can calculate, hydroponic farming only uses 10 percent as much land as conventional farming, less than 10 percent as much water, and can supply seven hundred households with fresh greens during the year.

Hydroponically grown, big, bright bouquets of fresh green and ruby red frilled leaf lettuce, peppery arugula, sturdy romaine, and fragrant bunches of basil are standouts in the aisles of the farmers' market. And with each purchase, you get a little something extra free of charge—the tangle of roots tied in a compact knot. Left attached, the lettuce will actually resist the urge to wilt readily, so it will have a better shelf life. What you won't get from hydroponic produce is dirt to wash off the leaves, a plus for the time-starved cook.

The harvest at Oasis Acres is continuous, predictable, and stretches the Ohio growing season well beyond nature's limits. Yet hydroponic farming challenges the Smuckers to think resourcefully—such as using a corn-burning furnace, fueled from their own field, to warm the greenhouse in the winter—and to keep a watchful eye every day of the year. "We're out here three times every day adjusting the pH levels in the water," says Glen. "They have to be just right so that the plants will easily absorb the minerals and nutrients, especially potassium and nitrogen, which make the lettuce sweet."

"Air and water temperature has to be just right, too—cool enough to grow but not so hot as to bolt and go to seed," he adds. "When you grow greens in the field, you can't as easily control Mother Nature."

Arugula Salad with Stone Fruit

Next to their fresh, peppery arugula, one of the hottest sellers from Oasis Acres is a cool blend of intensely colored green and red leaf lettuce that look like one compact head with distinctly separate leaves. Lois Smucker likes to think of it as an "already tossed salad" but admits its just two different seeds growing in the same "soilless" plug. "It's just a little something extra that gets the customer's attention," she says.

Makes 4 servings

Salad:

4 cups arugula, torn into bite-size pieces
4 cups red and green leaf lettuce, torn into bite-size pieces
½ cup thinly sliced red onion
2 ripe peaches, nectarines, or plums, pitted and sliced
2 tablespoons walnuts or pine nuts, toasted
¼ cup crumbled blue cheese

Dressing:

2 tablespoons cider vinegar, or any fruit-flavored vinegar
2 teaspoons brown sugar
1 teaspoon Dijon mustard
Salt and freshly ground black pepper
4 tablespoons extra-virgin olive oil

Combine the arugula, lettuce, red onion, and fruit in a large bowl. Toss and set aside.

In a small bowl, combine the vinegar, brown sugar, mustard, salt, and pepper. Whisk in the olive oil until completely blended.

Toss the dressing with the salad mixture. Divide among four salad plates and top with toasted nuts and crumbled blue cheese.

Spinach, Strawberry, and Dill Salad

Aside from the fresh sweet taste of hydroponically grown lettuce, the other benefit is that it's as clean as a whistle when it comes to the salad bowl. This salad takes advantage of the coinciding spring harvests of spinach and ruby red Ohio strawberries, and surprises the taste buds with sprigs of young dill.

Makes 6 servings

Salad:
8 cups fresh young spinach, washed
3 scallions, sliced thinly
½ cup hazelnuts, toasted
1 pint fresh strawberries, hulled and sliced
¼ cup chopped fresh dill

Dressing:
3 tablespoons red wine vinegar
1 tablespoon honey
2 cloves garlic, minced
1 teaspoon dry mustard
½ cup extra-virgin olive oil
Salt and freshly ground black pepper

In a large bowl, toss the spinach, scallions, hazelnuts, strawberries, and dill.

In a small bowl, combine the vinegar, honey, garlic, and mustard. In a slow, thin stream, whisk in the olive oil until blended. Season to taste with salt and pepper.

Just before serving, pour the dressing over the salad and toss to coat.

Basil Pesto and Basil Pesto Dipping Sauce

Pesto made with fresh tender basil leaves is a condiment that no kitchen should be without. Mix it into soups, stews, beans, and salad dressings; spread on grilled bread—the list goes on. And with some additional olive oil and a pinch of red pepper flakes, the basic recipe does double duty as a dipping sauce for crusty breads or freshly cut vegetables.

Makes 1¾ cups

2 cups packed fresh basil, stems removed, washed and dried
¾ cup freshly grated Parmesan cheese
½ cup pine nuts or walnut pieces
2 large cloves garlic, peeled
¼ teaspoon salt
¼ teaspoon freshly ground black pepper
⅔ cup extra-virgin olive oil

Using a food processor, combine all the ingredients except the olive oil and process until smooth. With the machine still running, slowly pour the olive oil through the chute in a slow, steady stream until combined. Store in an airtight container for up to a week, or freeze in small batches for up to 3 months.

To make a dipping sauce: Combine 3 tablespoons of the prepared pesto with ⅓ cup of olive oil and a pinch of crushed red pepper. Serve as a dipping sauce for crusty breads; sweet melons wrapped in ham; apples, pears, or whatever you desire.

THE ORCHARDS OF BILL AND VICKY THOMAS

Bill and Vicky Thomas
Zanesville, Ohio

The biggest challenge Bill and Vicky Thomas have in growing grapes isn't the birds or the bees or even the deer that like to nibble and sap the juicy ripe clusters on the vines—it's the customers. "When people think of seedless grapes, they think of the big, fat globes that come in from South America," says Vicky. "They don't even think that seedless homegrown grapes exist. Even then when they see the tight clusters of dime-size Ohio grown grapes, they don't regard them as adequate—until they taste them."

Bill and Vicky hand out plenty of samples of their grapes, four red seedless varieties and a seeded Concord in all, at the North Farmers' Market in Columbus. "We watch people take a few, walk away, and start thinking about their next purchase," she observes. "They hardly ever make it to the next booth before they head back to us wanting to know more about the grapes."

The Thomases farm a ten-acre orchard flanked by another forty acres thick with woods and picturesque views. When the couple bought the orchard, where Bill had worked as a youth, and moved their young family to these rolling hills, they dug right in, adding twenty-seven apple varieties, brambles, blueberries, plums—and tending a fickle peach orchard that went thirteen seasons without a profitable harvest. About the same time they were feeling the need to diversify, the Ohio Agricultural Research and Development Center (OARDC) approached the Thomases and twenty other farms throughout Ohio to grow seedless grapes, to see which varieties thrived in Ohio soil and weather. In exchange for an acre of grape vines, the Thomases made a five-year commitment to keep records and detailed observations about each aspect of growing grapes.

For the first three years, the couple planted, thinned, trimmed, and nurtured the vines, even creating a netting system that blanketed the entire vineyard to keep the birds out, although on occasion a determined one found its way in. By the third season, wonderful clusters of grapes swelled on the vines, with the promise of a good harvest. Timing is everything when it comes to harvesting, and grapes at their peak of quality and ripeness demand to be picked right about the same time school is called back into session. Bill, then a full-time teacher, returned to the classroom, and Vicky became a labor force of one. Almost single-handedly, she picked that first year's harvest of more than a thousand pounds. Each year that followed the yield grew, and by the time the vines were established, the average yield had reached six thousand pounds, with a banner year of ten thousand pounds.

It's been twenty years since the Thomases planted their vineyard. When Bill retired from teaching, their workforce doubled overnight, making the six-week harvest from late August through early October, although still hard work, more manageable. Of the twenty original experimental vineyards in Ohio, only the Thomases and a few others still produce grapes. "Grapes are more labor intensive than our orchard crops," admits Vicky. "They definitely started out as an experiment, but for our customers who come to buy apples, the grapes feel like a reward."

Grilled or Roasted Grapes

When Bill and Vicky Thomas are in the vineyard harvesting perfectly ripe grapes and the sun beats down warming the heavy clusters, they describe the scent as "intoxicating." Heat will do that to grapes, whether from the sun or the surface of a hot grill. Toss a cluster of Reliance seedless grapes on the grill and see how it enhances the delicate strawberry flavor with hints of spice.

Makes 4 to 6 servings

1 hearty bunch of seedless red Ohio grapes, such as Reliance or Mars variety, washed, dried and left as a cluster
4 sprigs fresh rosemary
Extra-virgin olive oil

Remove any shriveled or bruised grapes from the bunch. Tuck the sprigs of rosemary between the clusters and grapes. Lightly brush the surface of the grapes with olive oil.

Preheat the grill to medium-high or heat a grill pan over medium-high heat on the stove. Place the grapes on the cooking surface and grill on all sides, 2 to 3 minutes per side, until the grapes are warm and show a few grill marks. Transfer from the grill onto a plate. Serve with toasted baguettes, cheeses, and a glass of Pinot Noir.

Roasted Sausages with Grapes

Grapes roasted in the oven collapse to a pleasant jammy consistency resulting in an interesting side dish for the sausages. Choose an Ohio-grown Candadice, a small red seedless grape with a pronounced strawberry-like flavor; or Mars, a medium-size red seedless grape with a thicker skin. Serve with mashed potatoes or crusty bread to sop up the wonderful juices.

Makes 6 servings

3 pounds pork sausage, hot, sweet, or a combination
2 tablespoons unsalted butter
2 tablespoons extra-virgin olive oil
6 cups red seedless grapes
¼ cup balsamic vinegar

Fill a large stockpot with water and bring to a boil. Pierce the casings of the sausages with the tip of a knife and place them in the boiling water. Boil gently for about 10 minutes, drain, and set aside.

Preheat the oven to 450°F. Place a large roasting pan or heavy Dutch oven over medium-low heat. Heat the butter and olive oil until melted and bubbly. Add the grapes and toss to coat. Remove from the heat. Place the sausages among the grapes, pushing them down into the pan.

Roast for about 25 to 30 minutes until the sausages are browned and the grapes are soft and jam like. Using a slotted spoon, transfer the grapes and sausages to a warm serving platter.

Place the roasting pan over medium heat and add the vinegar, scraping the bottom of the pan to loosen the browned bits. Let the vinegar boil until reduced by half. Pour over the grapes and sausages, and serve immediately.

Grape and Rosemary Focaccia

In the vineyards at the Orchards of Bill and Vicky Thomas, the red seedless variety called Vanessa looks as good as it tastes with a blushing red, almost translucent skin. Its firm yet tender flesh melts smoothly on the tongue, releasing a sweet and tangy flavor. In this recipe, the grapes are baked into the bread, and that little extra kick of heat from the stove lifts them to the next level of sweetness.

Makes 8 servings

1 ounce active dry yeast
1¼ cups warm water (90°F–110°F)
3 cups plus 2 tablespoons all-purpose flour
1 teaspoon salt
2 tablespoons chopped fresh rosemary
1 tablespoon extra-virgin olive oil
1 cup seedless Ohio grapes, washed, dried, and stemmed
½ cup freshly grated Parmesan-Reggiano cheese
Coarse sea salt and freshly cracked black pepper

Stir the yeast into the warm water and let soften for 10 minutes.

Mix the flour, salt, and rosemary together in a large bowl. Make a well in the middle. Pour the oil into the well, followed by the water with the yeast. With a wooden spoon, mix the ingredients until they come together into a ball. Turn onto a floured surface and knead until the dough feels elastic, firm, and looks shiny. Sprinkle lightly with flour, and place in a lightly oiled bowl. Cover with plastic wrap and leave to rise in a warm place for 1 hour, or until doubled in size.

Preheat the oven to 425°F. Remove the dough from the bowl and place on a floured surface. Using your hands, stretch the dough into a 12-inch circle about ½-inch thick. Place on a baking sheet lined with parchment paper. Arrange the grapes over the surface of the bread and lightly press into the dough. Bake for 10 minutes. Sprinkle with Parmesan-Reggiano, salt, and pepper, and bake for an additional 10 minutes or until golden brown. Let cool slightly before serving.

RICH GARDENS ORGANIC FARM

Rich Tomsu and Ann Fugate
Shade, Ohio

Every spring, the great asparagus debate rages on: are thin stalks better than thick? It's the same question Rich Tomsu and Ann Fugate field season after season, when spring arrives at the Athens Farmers' Market. "Thicker is better," says Ann, repeating it so often it feels like a mantra. She illustrates her point by getting customers to think about how the green soldiers of spring grow as they push through the blanket of straw mulch.

"Asparagus sprouts out of the ground, fully formed, as thick and round as it's ever going to get," explains Ann. "The spears get taller, not thicker, the longer they spend in the soil. Thin spears have a greater proportion of tough outer skin, or rind cells [think of it as 'bark'], than tender inner cells. Thick spears have more of the succulent inner cells." That's the short answer, but the bottom line is that this argument only works when the asparagus is fresh. "When it's old, thick or thin," she add, "it's just old and tough."

The Tomsu's eighty-acre homestead and organic farm is tucked on a forested hillside where the view in every direction is of more thick woodlands and the gently sloping hills of Ohio's Appalachia. They farm on a fraction of their land that's "flat." "Even that's not really flat," says Rich. So they practice French intensive gardening, a method that runs on the modified principle "with less you really can get more." Less would refer to the heavy clay and shale that stand between determined farmers and a respectable crop.

French intensive, or "double dug" raised-bed gardening, a method originally developed for use in narrow backyards in France, translates well to the shale hills of Appalachia. Sections of raised beds are created by alternating layers of humus and compost until there is a two-foot-deep bed of light, airy, and nutritionally rich soil, seemingly custom built for the demanding nature of asparagus as well as the thirty varieties of lettuce, hardneck garlic, peppers, tomatoes, and potatoes that the Tomsus grow and harvest April through November.

When they moved to this little slice of heaven in 1975, Rich and Ann came with the intention to just live close to the land. Farming did not come naturally to Rich, a former English professor, or to Ann, a former health-care administrator. "We were from the suburbs," says Ann. "As far as we knew, God made concrete." Somewhere along the way, they began gardening—growing enough vegetables for them, and a bit more for friends and neighbors. The garden naturally grew into a productive certified organic farm in 1989.

"It was natural for us to farm organically," Rich says. "We didn't know what we were doing so we didn't have to 'unlearn' how to farm. We just farmed in a way that seemed right."

Asparagus with Tomatoes, Shallots & Pistachios

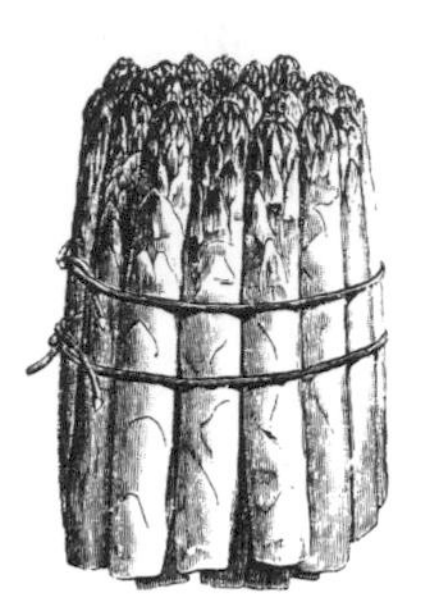

From their front porch, you can see the raised gardening beds that Rich Tomsu and Ann Fugate call Rich Gardens. But it's behind the house, past a thicket, that ranks of Jersey Giants stand at attention from April through May. "It's a super male asparagus variety that pays more attention to growing thick spears," said Rich, who asks that feminists please refrain from comment.

Makes 4 servings

1 pound asparagus, trimmed
½ stick unsalted butter
2 tablespoons minced shallots
1 large tomato, coarsely chopped
1 tablespoon fresh chopped parsley
1 teaspoon fresh lemon juice
Salt and freshly ground black pepper, to taste
¼ cup shelled, roasted pistachios, coarsely chopped

Bring a large pot of salted water to a boil. Add the asparagus spears and cook for 3 minutes until crisp tender. Drain well, cover, and set aside.

Melt the butter in a large heavy skillet. Add the shallots and sauté for 2 minutes until soft and transparent. Add the tomato, parsley, and lemon juice and heat thoroughly. Season to taste with salt and pepper.

To serve, divide the asparagus among four plates and spoon sauce over top. Sprinkle with the chopped nuts and serve immediately.

Roasted or Grilled Asparagus

There's a fine line between tough and tender asparagus—and that's right where the stalk snaps easily at the natural bend. Ann Fugate neatens the ends and stands them in a little water, keeping them fresh and moist until they reach the Athens Farmers Market on Saturday mornings. Within the first hour or so, the two-hundred one-pound bundles that took them a full day to pick will be gone, perhaps destined for the grill.

Makes 4 servings

1 pound fresh asparagus, washed and trimmed
3 to 4 tablespoons extra-virgin olive oil
Coarse salt and freshly ground black pepper
Balsamic vinegar (optional)

Brush the asparagus with the olive oil.

For oven roasting: Preheat the oven to 425°F. Arrange the oiled asparagus in a single layer in a shallow roasting pan. Roast for 8 to 10 minutes, until the asparagus is still crisp-tender and just beginning to brown. Remove from the oven, sprinkle with salt, pepper, and a splash of balsamic vinegar, if desired. Serve immediately.

To grill the asparagus: Place a grill basket or pan over the grill grate and heat the grill to medium-high. Place the oiled asparagus in the grill basket and grill until the asparagus is crisp-tender and just beginning to brown. Remove from the grill and sprinkle with salt, pepper, and a splash of balsamic vinegar, if desired. Serve immediately.

Asparagus with Red Peppercorn Dip

"Folks are always pleasantly surprised at the flavor and texture of really fresh asparagus," says Ann Fugate. She has personally witnessed the conversion of many skeptics at the Athens Farmers' Market as she hands them samples of fresh asparagus— firm stalks with a nutty texture and a fresh sweet taste akin to garden peas, a nice complement to the peppery floral tastes of this dip.

Makes about 1¼ cups dip

2 pounds fresh asparagus spears, trimmed if necessary

Dip:

1 cup sour cream
2 tablespoons buttermilk
1 tablespoon crushed red peppercorns
2 teaspoons chopped fresh chives
2 teaspoons chopped fresh thyme
1 clove garlic, finely minced
1 teaspoon salt

To blanch the asparagus spears, bring a large pot of salted water to a boil. Add the asparagus and cook for 2 to 3 minutes. Remove and plunge into an ice bath to shock the spears and stop them from cooking. Remove from the ice bath, drain, and dry. The spears should be crisp-tender and not limp.

To make the dip, place all of the ingredients in a small mixing bowl and stir to combine. Cover and place in the refrigerator for at least 2 hours or up to 48 hours, to allow the flavors to blend. Serve with fresh-from-the-garden asparagus spears, as well as other assorted garden-fresh vegetables such as cherry tomatoes, carrot sticks, and sweet peas.

SAGE'S APPLES AND SCHULTZ FRUIT FARM

Bob Sage
Chardon, Ohio

Gene "Bo" Schultz
Chesterland, Ohio

Gene "Bo" Schultz grew up on one of the greatest playground's a kid could hope for—his grandparents fifty-three-acre farm and apple orchard in Chesterland, that bears his surname. Finding a tree to climb was never a challenge. He attended Miami University in Oxford, served a hitch in the navy, and attended and graduated from Ohio State Agriculture School. Gene's grandmother sold him the farm on his word that he would still farm the land. With all the enthusiasm reserved for the young, Gene jumped into farming the family orchard with ambitious plans. After making a few mistakes and a handful of less-than-good choices, Gene admitted to himself that, while he may have grown up in an orchard, maybe he hadn't paid enough attention to how things were done. So he headed seven miles down the road for some sage advice.

Bob Sage of Sage's Apples is a fourth-generation apple farmer with a lifetime of orchard "know how"—and "know not to." From managing his own twenty-five acre orchard in Chardon at the side of his father and grandfather, and now with his brother and own son, he knows that lessons about farming and managing a productive orchard are not always the same ones learned from behind a desk. When it comes to farming, helping the guy next door who might be a competitor is not about revealing the secrets of your own success. "There's a lot of value in helping Gene find his own niche in farming," said Bob. "It's about nurturing the next generation of small family farms.

"Gene and I rubbed shoulders a lot at auctions when he was just beginning to farm," Bob says, "and he was full of questions." Bob was full of answers. "I probably told him more than he really wanted to know but I also didn't want him to repeat the same mistakes I've made." Between conversations on pest and disease control, storage equipment, and machinery, a friendship and mentorship developed.

Comparing apples to apples, Bob and Gene raise about twenty of the same varieties that whet the Ohio palate, including Lodi, Paula Red, Gala, Burgundy, Northern Spy, Holiday, Stayman, and Winesap. They both handpick their crop putting them in bins, not crates, just as both their families have for decades. Bob has helped Gene develop a good, sound practice for pest and disease control on his crops and helped him think through better solutions for storage.

"Gene is good at knowing who his market is," says Bob. "He knows what his customers want, what he can raise, and he's found lots of different marketing channels to go through." Bob sells his apples direct from his family farm market while Gene takes his harvest to area farmers' markets, where he's slowly building a reputation as the "go to" guy for obscure antique varieties, such as Newton Pippin, a squat, crisp yellow apple with a pine-like tartness that dates back to the 1700s; or Baldwin, a tart yellow apple mottled with red that until the 1920s was the most widely planted apple in the United States. Gene's ultimate goal is to have over a thousand trees in his orchard, filled with seventy-five new and heirloom varieties, a cider orchard and press, and his own on-farm market.

"People always talk about how farmers never make any money and struggle for a living," says Gene. "If I listened to that, I would be doing something else." Instead he's inspired by the success of family farms like the Sages'. One of the best lessons Gene has learned from farmers such as Bob Sage, and the best advice he has to pass along, is "When you need help, ask for it." And if you can help, do so generously.

Baked Apple Pancake

Gene Schultz has planted over twenty antique apple varieties, each with a unique history or story that makes them that much more interesting to eat. Esopus Spitzenburg is a firm, sweet apple with a pineapple flavor and a known favorite of Thomas Jefferson. Roxbury Russett is the oldest American apple variety, with a nectar-like flavor. Each is a good baking apple that holds its shape when cooked. Ohio-grown Melrose, Jonathan, or Winesap are good choices, too.

Makes 4 to 6 servings

4 tablespoons unsalted butter
3 apples, peeled, cored, and cut into thin wedges
1 cup all-purpose flour
1 cup milk
6 eggs
1 teaspoon vanilla
½ teaspoon salt
¼ teaspoon freshly grated nutmeg
Powdered sugar, to dust
Maple syrup, to accompany

Place a medium-size cast-iron skillet inside the oven and preheat the oven to 450°F while preparing the ingredients.

In another heavy skillet, melt 2 tablespoons of the butter over medium-high heat. Add the apples and sauté until they just begin to soften. Remove from the heat and set aside.

Place the flour, milk, eggs, vanilla, salt, and nutmeg in a blender or food processor and blend until thoroughly mixed.

Remove the cast-iron skillet from the oven and add the remaining 2 tablespoons of butter.

Arrange the sautéed apples evenly in the bottom of the skillet. Pour the batter over the apples. Return to the oven and bake for 15 minutes, then reduce the temperature to 375°F and bake an additional 10 minutes. Remove from the oven and let cool for 5 minutes. Dust with powdered sugar and cut into wedges. Serve immediately, passing the maple syrup.

Potato & Apple Galette

If you follow the varieties of apples as they ripen in the orchards at Sage's Apples and Schultz Fruit Farm, you could set your watch by the harvest. Beginning in late July, Lodi pie apples are the first to ripen, followed by Jersey Mac and Paula Reds in August. September begins with Honeycrisp, Elstar and Northern Spy apples and ends with Holiday, Ida Reds, and Granny Smiths. For this recipe, use firm, tart apples, such as Granny Smith.

Makes 6 to 8 servings

4 tablespoons extra-virgin olive oil
4 tablespoons unsalted butter, melted
4 large russet potatoes, scrubbed, and sliced thinly
2 large apples, peeled, cored, and sliced thinly
2 tablespoons minced fresh rosemary
Salt and freshly ground black pepper

Preheat the oven to 450°F. Brush a 9-inch round cake pan with a little of the oil and line the bottom with parchment paper. Butter the top of the parchment paper.

Combine the melted butter and the remaining olive oil. Place in a large bowl with the potato slices, apple slices, and rosemary. Toss to coat evenly. Sprinkle with salt and pepper, and toss again.

Layer the potato and apple slices in the prepared pan, overlapping the slices as you go. Pour any of the butter mixture that remains in the bowl over the top.

Bake until the potatoes are tender and pierce easily with the tip of a knife, about one hour. Remove from the oven. Wait 10 minutes, and then turn out onto a rimless baking sheet, removing the parchment paper. Place under the broiler for 2 to 3 minutes to brown the top. Transfer to a platter and cut into wedges. Serve immediately.

Apple & Sage Sauce

To call an apple variety "antique" simply means that it's been grown for a long time, dating back centuries and often originating from France, Holland, or England. The green-tinged Granny Smith arrived from Australia in the mid-1800s. Its firm texture and tart taste pairs naturally with the dusky sage and sweet maple syrup—and a grinding of fresh black pepper adds a wonderful component of heat. Serve this sauce with roasted pork, chicken, or turkey.

Makes 4 servings

3 tart apples, such as Granny Smith, peeled, cored, and cut into 1-inch pieces
3 tablespoons pure maple syrup
1 tablespoon water
Pinch of salt
1 tablespoon finely chopped fresh sage
Freshly ground black pepper, to taste

Combine the apples, maple syrup, water, and salt in a medium saucepan. Place over medium-low heat. Cover and cook for 15 minutes or until the apples become soft. Remove from the heat and mash the apple into a coarse sauce. Add the sage and pepper. Taste and adjust seasonings. Serve warm or at room temperature.

SHAFER'S PRODUCE

Harold Shafer and Family
Findlay, Ohio

As a child, Harold Shafer spent the summer of 1927 growing a melon in the family garden—a solitary melon, but still a source of pride for a seven-year-old. His father instructed him to put it on a potato crate alongside the road and sell it, which Harold did for a profit of ten cents. Harold's memory has faded. Many of the stories of his life as a farmer have been lost; others are no longer as clear. But he tells the story of how he earned his first dime with great detail; down to the model of the car that first customer drove. The coin, dated 1928, hangs on a chain around his neck, the first dime he ever earned farming the fields that have been his lifelong home and livelihood.

Harold is a patriarch of the Shafer family, now a fourth-generation farm family. The family has grown, so has the acreage, from a mere twenty-five acres in the early 1900s to over one thousand six hundred today, the majority of which grows wheat, beans, and field corn. In the statistical world of the United States Department of Agriculture, the Shafer's Hancock County farm does not qualify as a small farm. In fact, it is one of the largest in the state. Yet in theory and spirit, the Shafers run a small family farm that keeps them connected with their community and their customers.

Fifty acres amid the larger farming operation are dedicated to growing sweet corn, and another ten are dedicated to a variety of produce, including melons, tomatoes, cucumbers, squash, and pumpkins which they sell to friends and customers—many children, grandchildren, and great-grandchildren of a previous generation of buyers.

Harold's son and daughter, Judy and Joe, as well as their spouses, children, and grandchildren, all work the farm or in the on-farm market. On occasion, Harold will still drive the 1969 Massey Ferguson tractor from the field to the stand, hitched with a flatbed loaded with freshly picked corn and produce. It's not unusual for him to be greeted by groups of customers who show up early during the daily sweet corn harvest for the freshly picked ears with sugary names as sweet at the corn's taste: Temptation, Honey Select, and Precious Gem. For Harold, this is the part of farming he's loved from the very beginning—his customers.

A few years ago, the classic "big box" store went up down the road in what used to be productive farm fields. Whenever and wherever that happens, small business owners and farmers feel the threat of what "one-stop shopping" can do to their customer base. "You can go uptown for convenience," says Harold's daughter-in-law Cheryl, who, along with sister-in-law Judy, manages the market, "or out of town for farm fresh—the best you can get."

Corn on the Cob

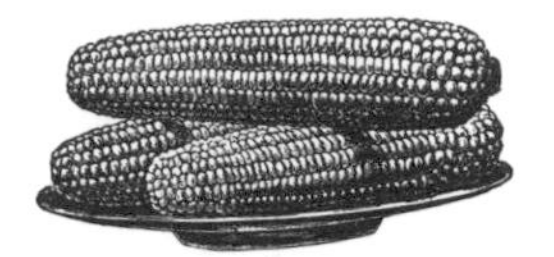

Ask Cheryl Shafer how to cook corn on the cob and she'll recite the classic recipe, a joke among corn farmers. "Pick the ear and run like mad back to the house where a pot of boiling water should be waiting," she says. The moment sweet corn is picked, the sugars begin to turn to starch and the kernels are on their way to becoming chewy. "The only way we really eat corn is from the field, off the cob, and sometimes without butter," says Cheryl. For the rest, here are three simple techniques to cooking corn on the cob.

Makes 6 servings

Grilled Corn

Leaving the husks and silks intact, submerge the corn in water, using a bucket or sink. Soak for at least 2 hours, or up to 6. When ready to cook, preheat the grill to medium high. Place the corn in a single row on the grill grate. Cook with the lid lowered for 15 to 20 minutes, turning every five minutes until lightly browned on all sides. To test for doneness, peel back the husk on one ear and press on a kernel. If it yields to pressure, the corn is done. Remove from grill. When ready to eat, the husks and silks will peel back easily.

Microwaved Corn

Make anywhere from one ear of corn to six. Remove the husks and silks. Place the cobs in a sealable gallon-size plastic bag, no more than six ears per bag. Seal the bag halfway. Place the bag on a plate and place it in the microwave. Set the timer for 2 minutes per ear. For example, if you have 6 ears, set the timer for 12 minutes; for 4 ears, 8 minutes. When done cooking, carefully remove the corn. Microwaves cook food from the inside out, so the corn will stay hotter longer than if prepared by other cooking methods.

Boiled Corn

Clean the corn by removing the husks and silks. Fill a large stockpot with water and bring to a boil. Place the ears in the boiling water and cook for 7 to 8 minutes. Remove and let cool slightly before serving.

Ohio Farmhouse Chowder

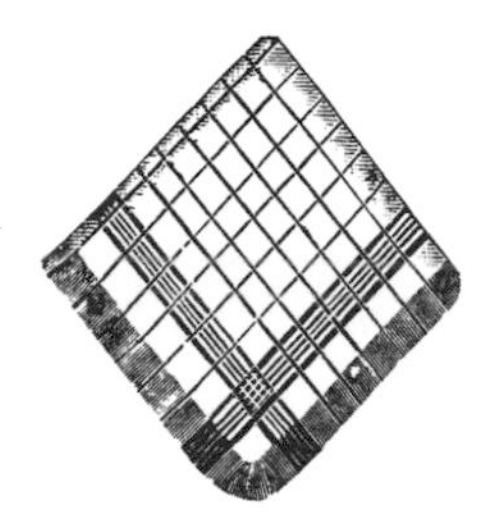

When the winter winds begin to blow, it's nice to have summer's sweet corn at hand for this farmhouse chowder. "We consider early varieties of sweet corn as eating corn," says Cheryl Shafer. "Later varieties are good for canning and freezing because they have a longer maturity date which allows the corn to develop more sugars." To freeze fresh sweet corn, simply cut from the cob and package in airtight plastic bags.

Makes 6 serving

3 slices thick-sliced bacon, chopped
2 cloves garlic, chopped
1 small onion, chopped
½ red bell pepper, chopped
4 cups chicken stock
2 cups cubed potatoes (½-inch cubes)
2 boneless, skinless chicken breast halves, cooked and chopped
2 cups corn kernels, removed from the cob (3 or 4 cobs)
1 tablespoon chopped fresh thyme
2 cups heavy cream
2 tablespoons chopped fresh parsley
Salt and freshly ground black pepper

In a large Dutch oven, cook the chopped bacon until crisp. Remove with a slotted spoon and set aside. Drain off all but 2 tablespoons of the bacon fat. Add the garlic, onion, and red bell pepper, and sauté over medium heat until soft, about 10 minutes. Add the chicken stock and bring to a boil. Add the cubed potatoes and cook until potatoes are soft and break apart easily with a fork, about 15 minutes.

Reduce heat to medium-low and add the chicken, corn, and thyme. Cook for 15 minutes. Add the cream and heat through without boiling. Stir in parsley and reserved bacon. Season to taste with salt and pepper. Let stand, or "cure," for an hour. Reheat gently, if necessary.

Corn, Bacon, and Sour Cream Casserole

The Shafers plant three successions of corn; in mid-April, May, and June, so that corn comes on starting in July and keeps coming through September, every day of the week. Canned corn can be substituted for fresh in this recipe, but make it a point to enjoy it just once during the season with kernels stripped from fresh-picked corn.

Makes 6 servings

3 cups fresh corn kernels, removed from the cob (4 to 5 cobs), or 3 (12-ounce) cans of corn, drained
2 tablespoons unsalted butter
2 tablespoons chopped onion
2 tablespoons all-purpose flour
8 ounces sour cream
½ teaspoon salt
6 slices thick-sliced bacon, cooked, drained, and crumbled

To cook the fresh corn kernels: Bring a large pot of water to a boil. Add ½ tablespoon of salt to the pot. Add the corn kernels and cook for 4 minutes. Drain and set aside.

Preheat oven to 350°F. In a large saucepan, melt the butter over medium-high heat. Add the chopped onion and sauté until soft and transparent. Add the flour and cook, stirring constantly for 1 minute. Add the sour cream and salt, and stir until blended. Remove from heat and add the corn and half the bacon, stirring until combined. Pour into a buttered 2-quart casserole. Top with the remaining bacon. Bake for 30 to 35 minutes, or until the top is slightly browned.

SIPPEL FAMILY FARM

Ben and Lisa Sippel
Mount Gilead, Ohio

When the dog days of summer roll around in central Ohio, temperatures in the fields can hit 95°F or better. Without even a tickle of a breeze, it can feel a lot hotter. In this kind of heat, vegetables in the fields at the Sippel Family Farm come on at a fast and furious pace. Harvesting won't wait for a break in the weather, and neither will customers who look forward to their fair share each week.

At twenty-six years old, Ben and Lisa are two of the youngest farmers in the state, committed to working their land and crops in ways that benefit the environment, their customers, and their sense of pride. Their seventy-seven acre farm, just north of Columbus, is part pasture for grass-fed beef, part hay, part green "manure," and twenty plentiful acres of naturally grown produce on their way to becoming organically certified. It's not surprising that, as farmers, they work every day, all year round. Their days are long and laborious and despite their youthfulness, their backs ache a little after a day in the fields.

"Some days we look around and wonder how we got here," says Lisa. "Other young married couples come home from work and go out at night, but we don't have a night life and we don't go on vacation." Ben and Lisa's lives revolve around the restrictions and demands of owning a farm, but Lisa is quick to add, with a satisfied tone, that, "We chose to do this—it didn't just happen to us."

Ben, an environmental studies graduate from Ohio Wesleyan, and Lisa, a middle school teacher throughout the academic year and a self-proclaimed "slave" in the summer, operate their farm as a CSA—community supported agriculture, an innovative concept developed in Japan and Switzerland in the 1960s that took hold in the United States in the mid 1980s. In a CSA arrangement, the farmer and customer join together in a small-scale economic partnership. In order to run a profitable farm, the Sippels need committed, dependable customers for their crops. So they sell annual shares in the Sippel Family Farm. In return, Ben and Lisa supply their customers with healthy portions of high-quality produce that they farm for about thirty weeks out of the year.

"Joining a CSA is like buying a CD at the bank," explains Ben. "There's a return on your investment, also a small risk, such as weather conditions that might wipe out or reduce a crop. The loss is ours in terms of time, seed, and tending, but we plant enough to make sure our customers are always supplied." It's a reliable way for young farmers such as the Sippels to have a secure business outlook.

Beginning in late March, Ben and Lisa distribute bins of freshly harvested produce each week to their CSA members from a central location, starting with the first-of-the-season fresh salad greens from their greenhouse. In early spring, it's sweet scallions, crunchy radishes, tender spinach, and heavy heads of cabbage. A few weeks later, it's sweet snap peas. Come summer, zucchini, peppers, eggplants, and a mix of heirloom tomatoes are in abundance, and so it goes until the first frost shuts down the growing season. The last bins, filled with pumpkins, potatoes, squashes, onions, shallots, and broccoli arrive just in time for their customers' Thanksgiving tables.

"We think we're successful," says Lisa. "We like what we're doing and we like knowing who's eating our vegetables. It's better than taking them to a store and not knowing who's eating it or what they are doing with it or even if they are enjoying it." Among their CSA members are the couple's dentist and physician. "We take care of one another's health," says Lisa. "Sometimes we get invited to parties where our members serve our vegetables," she adds. "Not that we can always go, but it still makes us part of this special community."

Heirloom Spaghetti Sauce

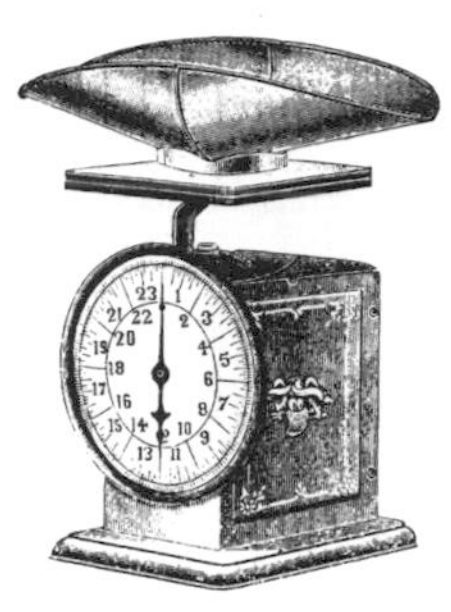

In Lisa Sippel's recipe for Heirloom Spaghetti Sauce, she recommends "mixing and matching" colors and varieties of tomatoes, making sure to include the meatier paste tomatoes. Be sure to enjoy the way the maple syrup balances the acidity of the tomatoes and imparts a subtle, smoky flavor.

Makes about 3 quarts

¼ cup extra-virgin olive oil
2 medium yellow onions, chopped
2 cloves garlic, minced
5 pounds Heirloom tomatoes, diced
¼ cup maple syrup
Salt and freshly ground black pepper

Place a large skillet over medium-high heat. Heat the olive oil. Add the onions and garlic, and sauté until soft and transparent, 8 to 10 minutes. Add the chopped tomatoes and stir to combine. Reduce the heat to low and simmer for 45 minutes to an hour, until thick and reduced in volume. Add the maple syrup and cook an additional 10 minutes. Season to taste with salt and pepper. Toss the sauce with cooked spaghetti noodles, or cool and refrigerate for up to 1 week, reheating when needed. This sauce can be frozen in tightly sealed containers or freezer bags.

Japanese Eggplant Spread

Ben and Lisa Sippel love to educate their customers about new uses for fresh vegetables, such as Japanese eggplants. Long, slender, and ranging in color from lavender and pink to green and white, Japanese eggplants have thin skins, few seeds, and a delicate flavor. Lisa also uses this spread as a pizza-style sauce on thick pita bread, topped with black olives, roasted red peppers, red onion, and crumbled feta. Warm it in the oven and serve.

Makes 2 cups

3 Japanese eggplants, or one medium black bell eggplant, unpeeled, diced into ¼-inch cubes
1 large tomato, diced into ¼-inch cubes
1 small onion, diced into ¼-inch cubes
1 or 2 jalapeño peppers, finely diced (see tip)
5 tablespoons extra-virgin olive oil, plus extra if needed
Salt and freshly ground black pepper

Preheat oven to 400°F. Toss the diced eggplant, tomato, onion, and jalapeño with the olive oil. Spread in a single layer on a baking sheet and sprinkle with salt and pepper. Roast, stirring occasionally, for 20 minutes, until soft and lightly browned. Remove and let cool for 5 minutes.

Place the roasted vegetables in a food processor and process until smooth. Add additional olive oil if the mixture appears dry. Season to taste with salt and pepper.

Tip: To control the heat of the jalapeño, remove the seeds and membrane before roasting.

Rainbow Salt Potatoes

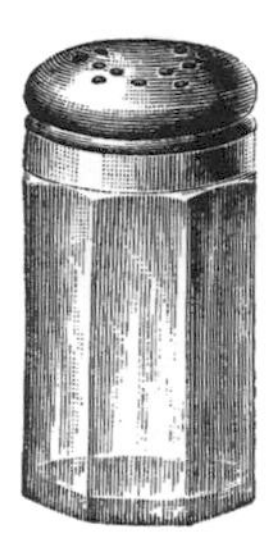

A potato is truly "new," not just small, if you can peel off the parchment-like skins with your fingers. They won't store as well as large spuds, so they should be used within a few days of buying them. Their high moisture content and creamy texture make them good choices for cooking whole. This easy recipe is short on ingredients but long on flavor.

Makes 6 servings

2 pounds uniform-size mixed new potatoes (red, white, or purple), scrubbed clean and left whole
¼ cup kosher or sea salt
4 tablespoons unsalted butter, melted
Freshly cracked black pepper

Fill an 8-quart saucepan with water and bring to a rolling boil. Add ¼ cup of salt. Pierce each potato with a fork. Add the potatoes to the boiling water and cook until a fork pierces through easily, about 15 minutes. Drain the potatoes, but do not rinse. The potatoes will have a pale white salt powder on them. Toss in the butter, season to taste with pepper, and serve warm.

Lavender Roasted Vegetables

When using lavender for cooking or roasting, look for early blooming English varities, specifically angustifolia. Its sweet, floral flavor features hints of lemon, citrus, and mint. Two teaspoons is just the right amount of this potent herb to rise above the medley of hearty roasted vegetables.

Makes 6 to 8 servings

2 teaspoons fresh English lavender
½ teaspoon salt
¼ teaspoon cracked black pepper
1½ pounds small red potatoes, quartered
1 pound carrots, cut into 1-inch chunks
½ pound small white onions, peeled
3 garlic cloves, minced
2 tablespoons olive oil
2 small zucchini, cut into ½ inch slices

Preheat oven to 400°F. In a small bowl, combine the lavender, salt, and pepper. In a large bowl, toss the potatoes, carrots, onions, and garlic with the olive oil and half of the lavender mixture. Spread on a shallow baking sheet and roast for 25 minutes. Stir in the zucchini and sprinkle with the remaining lavender mixture. Roast 10 additional minutes until vegetables are soft.

FINDING A NICHE

A NICHE IS A VERY SMALL PLACE in the grand scheme of farming. Sometimes the land determines the niche. Bud Luers found his niche in the hundreds of nuts trees, purposely planted on his property long before he arrived. For Chris Chmiel, a passionate pawpaw farmer, the peculiar fruit grows abundantly wild on his acreage in southern Ohio.

For others, the niche comes as a legacy, such as Ron Franklin's maple farm, first tapped by his great-grandfather, or Shelia and Denzil St. Clair's honey farm that began as a dowry of bees.

Still others create their niche by growing something that will distinguish them from all others. They become the "go-to" farmer for something as exotic as wild mushrooms or gourmet garlic varieties.

Perhaps one of the most interesting aspects of niche farming is that it often plays a great role in preserving a dwindling crop such as black walnuts, or reviving a homestead art such as brewing hard cider.

For some, farming a niche can be a profitable, sustainable way of life or a profitable hobby. For certain though, success is not always reflected in the bottom line but in just being unique.

FRANKLIN'S TALL TIMBERS

Ron Franklin
Ashtabula, Ohio

One of the best testimonials for Ron Franklin's maple syrup is a story about a four-year-old customer—a little boy with a highly developed palate for pure maple flavor. One Sunday, the boy's mother presented him with a short stack and a bottle of imitation maple-flavored syrup. "Where's the maple syrup?" he asked her. When she told him they had run out, he politely pushed the pancakes aside and asked, "Well then, can I have cereal?"

It's not that Ron's recipe for maple syrup is a closely guarded secret. "It's fifty gallons of sap, a pound of smoke, and a teaspoon of ash," he says in jargon only understood by sugar makers who boil their syrup over a wood fire. It's just that you can't fake real maple syrup, a fine balance of natural flavor and sweetness.

When you walk into the thick of Ron's ninety-five acre sugar bush that he calls Franklin's Tall Timbers, you quickly realize that technology has squeezed out the familiar bucketing methods portrayed in Currier and Ives prints—the same method used for over eighty years and three generations of Ron's family. While more than 60 percent of Ohio's eight-hundred maple syrup producers still use the labor-intensive bucketing method where the maples are tapped, and the sap flows into a bucket that is hauled many times over to the sugar shack, a growing number, including Ron, find tubing or "pipelines" a necessary way to expedite collection and reduce the cost of labor.

Miles and miles of white plastic tubing, reminiscent of empty clotheslines, connect over 3,200 Ohio sugar maples at Franklin's Tall Timbers to a centrally located pump house. Ron keeps a close eye on the weather, not the calendar, for a sign for when to begin syrup collection. When the days warm to thirty-five degrees or better but the nights still drop back to freezing, Ron is quick to flip the switch. The powerful vacuum pump begins to draw the sap from the maples through the tubes into the pump house and out a faucet, quickly filling the collection tank much as one would fill a bathtub. From the pump house, dwarfed by century-old maples, the sap travels over one mile through an underground pipeline to the sugar shack. When the sap is flowing freely the pump can run all day, drawing 18,000 gallons of sap.

While the efficiency of tubing has taken the "romance" out of collecting sap, not much has changed in the way Ron processes the thin, watery sap into rich Grade A Ohio maple syrup. It takes about four hours and a hot wood fire to boil one thousand five hundred gallons of the colorless liquid into thirty gallons of thick, sweet syrup. By the end of the three to six weeks that characteristically make up maple syrup season, Ron will have bottled one thousand gallons of syrup. It's a short but sweet season filled with interrupted sleep and long, arduous days. Once in a great while, Ron encounters a customer who balks at the price tag on real Ohio maple syrup. A walk through the woods and the process, from tap to bottle, is a humbling lesson that can loosen the grip on even the most tight-fisted customer.

A good season for Ron pays off in a variety of ways other than the flow of the sap and the yield of syrup. Sightings of deer and their wobbly legged fawns, fox, and wild turkey, and conversations with his children and grandchildren among the tall, tall timbers rank high among the most important measures of a perfect maple sugar season.

Maple Walnut Tart

All maple syrup is sweet, but in different measures. Grade A light amber syrup has a smooth and delicate flavor. Made from the sap collected early in the season, it has a higher concentration of sugar requiring less processing to make syrup. For this Maple Walnut Tart, the result is a pleasant, not cloyingly, sweet taste.

Makes 8 to 12 servings

Crust:

2 cups all-purpose flour
2 tablespoons sugar
½ teaspoon salt
¼ teaspoon baking powder
½ cup unsalted butter, diced and chilled
⅓ cup vegetable shortening, diced and chilled
6 tablespoons ice water, plus extra if needed

Filling:

3 eggs
1 cup Grade A light amber maple syrup
¾ cup packed light brown sugar
2 tablespoons unsalted butter, melted
1 teaspoon vanilla extract
½ teaspoon salt
1 cup coarsely chopped walnuts
Whipped cream (optional)

To make the crust: In a large bowl, combine the dry ingredients. Use a pastry blender to cut in the butter and shortening until the butter pieces are the size of small peas. Add the ice water and toss with a fork until the mixture comes together. Gather into a ball, flatten, and wrap in plastic wrap. Refrigerate for one hour. Roll the dough out on a floured surface to fit a 12-inch tart pan. Press the dough into the tart pan and trim the excess dough. Place in the freezer for 30 minutes.

Preheat the oven to 425°F.

To make the filling: In a medium-size bowl, combine the eggs, maple syrup, brown sugar, butter, vanilla, salt, and nuts.

Remove the shell from the freezer and pour the maple syrup mixture into the shell. Bake for 25 to 30 minutes, until the crust is golden and the filling is soft-set. Let stand for one hour before serving with a dollop of whipped cream.

Autumn Salad With Maple Vinaigrette

Grade A medium and dark amber syrups are from sap collected later in the season, before the maples begin to bud. They have less sugar than the early harvest so they need more time over the fire. The result is thicker, darker syrup with a more robust flavor which is just what this vinaigrette calls for.

Makes 4 servings

Salad:

1 head romaine lettuce, washed and torn into bite-sized pieces
2 tart apples, such as Granny Smiths, cored and thinly sliced
½ red onion, cut into thin rings
Salt and freshly ground black pepper, to taste
½ cup crumbled blue cheese
½ cup chopped walnuts or pecans, toasted

Maple Vinaigrette:

1 teaspoon dry mustard
½ teaspoon dried basil
¼ cup cider vinegar
½ cup pure maple syrup
1 tablespoon lemon juice
1 clove garlic, minced
1 cup extra-virgin olive oil
Salt and freshly ground black pepper, to taste

Chill 4 salad plates. In a large bowl, combine the lettuce, apple slices, and red onion. Season with salt and pepper. Set aside.

To prepare the vinaigrette: Combine the dry mustard, basil, vinegar, syrup, lemon juice, and garlic in a small bowl. Add the olive oil in a slow, steady stream, whisking constantly. Season with salt and pepper to taste. Pour enough dressing over the salad mixture to coat and toss.

Divide the salad between the plates. Top each with the crumbled blue cheese and chopped nuts, passing the additional dressing. Serve immediately.

Crispy Maple Spareribs

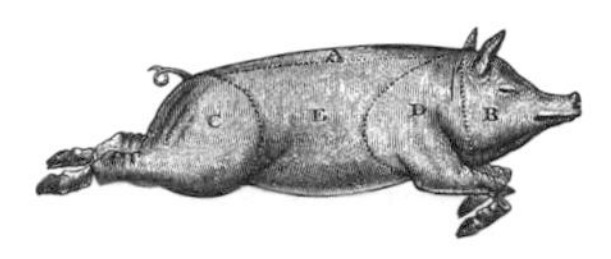

This simple sauce is sweet and sticky and oh so "maple-y." It leaves a caramelized-like crust on the meat that adds a little welcome crunch. Be sure to only use the sauce during the last five minutes of cooking as sauces heavy with sugars tend to burn quickly. The sauce can be made up to a week in advance and refrigerated until needed.

Makes 4 to 6 servings

2 to 3 pounds pork spareribs
Salt and freshly ground black pepper

Maple Sauce:
½ cup pure maple syrup
1 tablespoon chili sauce
1 tablespoon Worcestershire sauce
1 tablespoon red wine vinegar
1 small onion, minced
½ teaspoon dry mustard
Salt and freshly ground black pepper, to taste

Preheat the oven to 325°F. Season the spareribs with salt and black pepper. Loosely wrap each rack of ribs in aluminum foil. Place on a baking sheet. Bake for 1½ to 2 hours until ribs are tender. Remove and let cool for 30 minutes.

Meanwhile, combine all of the ingredients for the sauce in a saucepan and bring to a boil. Let boil for 5 minutes. Remove from heat and let sit at room temperature.

To finish the ribs, brush the meatier side of the ribs generously with half of the sauce. Place the ribs, sauced side down on a hot grill, or sauced side up 6-inches under a hot broiler, for about 5 minutes until the sauce is bubbly and caramelized. Turn the ribs over, brushing the other side with the remaining sauce. Continue to cook for a few minutes more. Remove from the heat and let cool slightly before separating the individual ribs with a knife.

INTEGRATION ACRES

Chris Chmiel
New Albany, Ohio

Chris Chmiel does not aspire to be the Pawpaw "King" of Ohio, but he will settle for the title of the Pawpaw "Kid," a title befitting this youthful, spirited southern Ohio farmer who works tirelessly growing, promoting and educating the public about possibly the most obscure fruit in Ohio—the pawpaw.

"The pawpaw was around long before the apple showed up," says Chris, who farms the fruit on his fifty-acre farm, Integration Acres. "It was eaten by Native Americans, and Lewis and Clark lived on it during their expeditions when their other provisions ran out." The peculiar fruit has been growing in wild stands in the southern Ohio area for hundreds of years and has a presence in almost every state east of the Mississippi. Yet few beyond the reaches of these patches recognize or have ever experienced the fruit outside of folk tunes like "Way Down Yonder in the Pawpaw Patch," or as the object of a bear's desire in Rudyard Kipling's *The Jungle Book*. "It has an unfamiliar look," says Chris, "and it is an acquired taste."

Nicknamed the "poor man's banana" or "custard apple," the egg-shaped fruit has a delicate green hide that develops blotchy dark patches as it ripens, although the "locals" and true fans of the fruit consider the flavor at its best when the skin ripens to black. Cut into one and the flesh can range in color from a pale yellow to a neon-like orange with as few as a half dozen or as many as two dozen seeds the size of apricot pits, and with a consistency that ranges from creamy and silky to thick and viscous. The aroma is unique and sweet, with a heavy tropical perfume and taste that Chris describes as a blend of melon, banana, and pineapple, ranging in intensity from mild to pungent, dependent on the growing season and time of harvest, which runs from mid-August to early October.

As a pawpaw grower, Chris serves an exclusive niche market with elusive products from Integration Acres, produced using natural and organic farming methods. He grows and harvests a variety of culinary plants and products native to the Appalachian forests of southern Ohio such as black walnuts, the elusive morel mushrooms, spicebush berries, goldenseal, and ginseng, all while continually expanding his pawpaw patch with new plantings. Still, chances are that it is rare to come across a pawpaw in the grocery store and there is only a slightly better chance of spotting one at a farmers' market. Each year, Chris harvests and ships about five hundred pounds of pawpaws and processes another two thousand for their pulp, which he sells frozen or processes into jams, sauces, and chutneys. Each year, he sells out by mid-October.

Every chance he gets, Chris promotes pawpaws, whether as an active member of the Ohio Pawpaw Growers Association or as the creator of the Ohio Pawpaw Festival, which draws thousands of visitors every September to Lake Snowden in southern Ohio, featuring pawpaw beer and wine, a pawpaw cook-off, and a pawpaw eating contest. He is the Pawpaw Kid on a mission.

Chris sees great potential and a special place of honor for the pawpaw in Ohio. He's out to make history, circulating petitions and asking pawpaw lovers to contact their state representatives to have the pawpaw named the state fruit. "That would certainly set us apart from any other state," he says confidently.

Sweet, Hot, and Tangy Barbecue Sauce

Pawpaws definitely add the sweet component to this unique barbecue sauce. Slather it on ribs or chicken during the final few minutes of grilling.

Makes 2 cups

1 head garlic, peeled and separated into cloves
1 onion, peeled and quartered
2 tablespoons extra-virgin olive oil
1 large tomato, peeled, seeded, and chopped
1 apple, peeled, cored, and chopped
1 jalapeño pepper, seeded and chopped
2 long green hot peppers, seeded and chopped
½ cup apple cider vinegar
1 tablespoon brown sugar
½ teaspoon paprika
½ teaspoon Worcestershire sauce
½ teaspoon achiote paste*
1 cup fresh or frozen pawpaw pulp

Preheat the oven to 400°F. Place the garlic and onion in a large bowl. Add the olive oil and toss to coat. Spread on a shallow baking tray and bake for 20 to 30 minutes, stirring once or twice, until soft and lightly browned. Remove and let cool.

Place all the ingredients except the pawpaw pulp in a large saucepan and cook over low heat for about 45 minutes, until the apples and chili peppers are soft. Remove from heat and add the pawpaw pulp. Place in a food processor or blender and process until smooth. Return to the saucepan and simmer for 5 minutes. Season to taste with salt and pepper.

*Achiote paste is available in the Hispanic food section of many markets.

Pawpaw Lassi

Casa Nueva restaurant in Athens, Ohio, uses Integration Acres' frozen pawpaw pulp for the "Appalachian" version of this traditional Indian yogurt beverage. The tang of the yogurt offsets the sweetness of the pawpaw perfectly.

Makes 4 servings

½ cup ice-cold water
4 cups plain yogurt
⅔ cup honey
½ teaspoon salt
1 cup frozen pawpaw pulp
½ teaspoon ground cinnamon

Place all the ingredients in a blender and process until smooth. Pour into tall glasses and serve immediately.

KILLBUCK VALLEY MUSHROOMS

Tom and Wendy Wiandt
Burbank, Ohio

There's a lot that sets Tom and Wendy Wiandt apart from other small family farmers in Ohio. On their forty-six acre farm in northeast Ohio, there are no fields to tend, they don't worry about too much or too little rainfall or sunshine, and they raise and harvest a unique product year round. They are genuinely modest, easy-going, and earthy yet have a flair for the exotic and wild—mushrooms, to be exact.

In 2002, Tom and Wendy both walked away from the comfort of steady paychecks, he as a mechanical engineer and she as a medical technologist, and into the world of fungi, clearly a specialty crop and one that their science backgrounds prepared them well to undertake.

Since then, they have produced a steady harvest of cultivated mushroom varieties, such as shiitake, Lion's Mane or "mock lobster," and oyster mushrooms in shades of white, pink, gold, brown, and dusky blue, and a seasonal, wild harvest of porcini, morels, and golden chanterelles from the organically certified woods that is their "farm."

In the woods, nature does the sowing, nurturing, and growing for the wild varieties but when it comes to cultivated varieties, the Wiandts have it down to a science. The process begins in Wendy's workshop, a small laboratory filled with test tubes and cultures of mycelia and mushroom spawn. She places a small chunk of the mycelia into a malt sugar solution, where after about two weeks it shows signs of life, thick and bubbly, much like proofing yeast. The broth is then mixed with sterilized rye grain and held at a controlled temperature for another two weeks, until the mycelia have spawned, or created a white fibrous matter. Tom steps in to mix the spawn with pasteurized straw and packs it into clear cylindrical plastic bags called "columns," each about five feet long, which he hangs from the ceiling of a small incubator room like neat rows of punching bags.

In a few weeks, the columns are moved to rooms where the environment mimics that of the warm and moist forest floor, and the mushrooms begin to fruit out of the holes poked in the bag. Beautiful exotic shapes, some tall and slender, others compact and full, will cover the surface of the bags that Tom and

Wendy will harvest twice daily. The mushrooms will fruit another four times in the next two months before the spent column is replaced with a fresh one, continuing the cycle. Chemicals to control pests or disease are out of the question. Instead the Wiandts opt for putting their efforts into maintaining a hygienic environment and controlling the occasional pest with a watchful eye, sticky traps, and by hand.

Outside the incubator building, the Wiandts have assembled a "patch" of decaying logs harvested from the woods surrounding their acreage. They inoculate the logs with mycelium and have been experimenting with growing a seasonal crop of shiitake mushrooms.

Every Saturday, the couple takes bushels of near-perfect, freshly harvested mushrooms to the North Union Farmers' Markets, Wendy heading west to the Westlake Crocker Park site and Tom traveling east to the square in Shaker Heights. Although Killbuck Valley Mushrooms carry a premium price tag, Tom and Wendy still leave the markets with empty bushel baskets each week.

"The farmers' markets are where we promote our mushrooms the best," said Tom. "Even though they are featured on some restaurant menus around Cleveland, the farmers' markets are where people really get to know us and we get to know our customers. It's where they can learn about and experience the unique tastes of mushrooms they might not be familiar with."

Shiitake and Black Walnut Stuffing

The firm texture of shiitake mushrooms are perfect in recipes calling for long cooking times such as this one. Their strong flavor won't be overwhelmed by the equally strong flavor of Ohio's black walnuts.

Makes 12 servings

1 pound sourdough bread, cut into ½-inch cubes
1 pound shiitake mushrooms, tough stems discarded, finely chopped
1 tablespoon freshly minced garlic
2 tablespoons extra-virgin olive oil
1 cup chopped leeks
¼ cup chopped black walnuts
1½ tablespoons chopped fresh thyme
1 tablespoon chopped fresh sage
4 tablespoons chopped fresh parsley
8 eggs
4 cups heavy cream
2 teaspoons salt
¼ teaspoon freshly ground pepper
6 ounces goat cheese (about 1 cup)

Preheat oven to 250°F. Spread the bread cubes on a baking sheet and toast for 20 minutes, stirring once. Remove the pan from the oven and increase the oven temperature to 325°F. Grease a 9 x 13-inch baking dish. Set aside.

Sauté the mushrooms and garlic in the olive oil for 10 minutes.

In a large bowl, toss together the bread cubes, mushrooms, leeks, black walnuts, thyme, sage, and half the parsley.

In a separate bowl, whisk together the eggs, heavy cream, salt, and pepper. Drizzle over the bread mixture, tossing and stirring constantly until all the liquid is absorbed evenly. Pack lightly into the prepared baking dish. Crumble the goat cheese over the top and cover with foil.

Bake for 40 minutes. Remove the foil and bake for an additional 30 minutes, or until golden. Garnish with the remaining parsley.

Sautéed Oyster Mushrooms and Fingerling Potato Salad

Oyster mushrooms are the fastest growing variety at Killbuck Valley Mushrooms, going from spawn to harvest in about two weeks. In addition to their fanned caps and deeply ridged gills, they are delicate in flavor and best when sautéed briefly with other mild-tasting ingredients including gently flavored herbs.

Makes 6 servings

2 pounds fingerling potatoes
5 tablespoon extra-virgin olive oil
1 onion, thinly sliced
2 pounds oyster mushrooms
6 cloves garlic, minced
1 tablespoon balsamic vinegar
½ cup chopped fresh parsley
Salt and freshly ground black pepper

Place the potatoes in a large pot and add water to cover. Bring to a boil and cook until fork tender. Drain and let cool slightly. Cut into quarters. Transfer to a large bowl.

Heat 2 tablespoons of the oil in a large skillet. Add the onion and sauté until golden brown and soft, about 10 minutes. Add to the potatoes.

Add 2 more tablespoons of the oil to the skillet, and the mushrooms and garlic, and sauté until soft and tender, about 5 minutes. Add to the potato mixture.

Drizzle the potato mixture with the remaining 1 tablespoon of olive oil, balsamic, and parsley. Season to taste with salt and pepper. Toss lightly before serving.

Tomato Porcini Sauce with Noodles

Tom and Wendy Wiandt harvest porcini mushrooms from the woods at Killbuck Valley Mushrooms around August, if there has been enough rainfall—if it's dry, there is no harvest. Porcinis are a smooth, moist mushroom with an umbrella shape and an earthy rust color. There's nothing mild about the flavor of this mushroom, so you'll want to use it in recipes that welcome big, earthy tastes.

Makes 4 servings

¼ cup extra-virgin olive oil
1 pound fresh porcini mushrooms, stems removed and sliced
4 cloves garlic, coarsely chopped
Salt and freshly ground black pepper, to taste
2 cups diced fresh tomatoes
¼ cup chicken or vegetable stock
¼ cup chopped fresh flat-leaf parsley
1 pound broad egg noodles, cooked and drained
Freshly grated Parmigiano-Reggiano cheese, to taste

Heat 2 tablespoons of the olive oil in a large skillet over medium-high heat. Add half of the mushrooms and garlic. Season with salt and pepper and cook until slightly softened and lightly browned, about 3 to 4 minutes. Transfer to a plate. Repeat with the remaining oil, mushrooms, and garlic. Add to the reserved mushrooms.

Add the tomatoes to the skillet and cook until some of the liquid has been released, about 4 to 5 minutes. Add the chicken stock and parsley and continue to simmer over medium heat for another minute. Season to taste with salt and pepper. Return the mushrooms to the skillet and heat through. Add the cooked noodles to the skillet, tossing gently to coat. Add grated cheese to taste. Serve immediately, passing extra cheese, if desired.

LUERS NUT FARM

Bud Luers
Bellville, Ohio

For the sake of expediency, it needs to be said right away: Bud Luers lives on a nut farm. At least that's what the flag at the end of the drive says—that and hundreds of nut trees that obscure the view of his house from the road. Nut farming, in the grand scheme of Ohio agriculture, is niche farming. That might be a more sophisticated description than Bud, a retired General Motor's employee, would prefer to attach to being a nut farmer. Still it's a title befitting someone who takes great personal care in how his product is grown and handled—one nut at a time.

Luers Nut Farm sits on Opossum Run Road, just outside of Mansfield. "This is not the best place in Ohio to grow nuts," Bud admits. It was, however, a great place to raise seven children with his wife, Marilyn, and to nurture his nut-growing hobby into a small business. Opossum Run Road winds through a small valley and has been described by local meteorologists as the coldest spot in the state—often twelve degrees lower than neighboring Mansfield. That makes Bud's nut trees vulnerable to the earliest and latest frosts recorded in the state, which puts the blossoms on the nut trees in a precarious position, having more than once wiped out a potential crop of Persian Walnuts or Northern Pecans. Chestnuts are rarely a worry, as they won't bloom until June, when the danger of frost has passed.

On Bud's nut farm are 350 grafted trees bearing nut fruits, including the delicate butternut; the familiar Chinese chestnut, a close cousin to the American chestnut; hazelnuts, more commonly known as filberts; hickories and hicans, a pecan hybrid; and heartnuts, a mild Japanese butternut that, when split along the seam and spread open, reveals a mild-tasting nut tucked inside a perfectly heart-shaped shell.

Among all the nut varieties Bud grows, none is more dependable than the black walnut, a native Ohio species with a strong, slightly bitter flavor. The more they age, or dry, in the hull, the stronger they get. Can a nut be too strong? Only if they are not shelled shortly after they fall. If that's the case, "Well, they'll take the hide off your tongue," warns Bud.

There are one hundred grafted black walnuts among the rows of nut trees and another six hundred seedlings scattered throughout the twenty-six wooded areas that surround his home. As the nuts ripen, a sporadic round of thuds can be heard round the clock for weeks, as the heavy green hulls fall seventy feet to the ground. Bud collects them on a daily basis with a nut collector, called a 'Nut Wizard,' a simple contraption powered by his motivation to avoid bending over or crawling around to harvest the fallen nuts. It closely resembles a bingo cage attached to the end of a long stick. As Bud rolls the cage over the hulls, they squeeze themselves between the flexible tines and collect inside.

After the nuts have spent a couple of weeks drying inside their beautifully rippled shells it's time for Bud to get crackin'... literally, one nut at a time, with what looks like a giant pedal-powered nutcracker converted from an old brake-riveting machine. Bud places a nut in a little cup on the machine, and from years of practice, applies just the right amount of foot pressure to split the shells, leaving the nutmeats intact. Bud will crack every nut he harvests with his only tools: his "cracker foot" and a hand-held nipper to pry stubborn shells apart. "The only thing I have to worry about breaking down is me," he jokes.

Luers Nut Farm is likely the largest nut producer in the state of Ohio. When Bud puts pencil to paper and compares the hours he puts into nut farming against the sales of the hand-cracked nuts, he figures he's working for minimum wage—but getting paid in maximum enjoyment.

Aunt Jane's Black Walnut Refrigerator Cookies

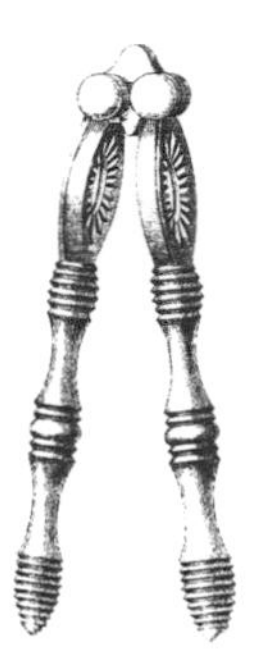

Black walnuts are appreciated most by Bud's more "mature" customers. "They are a nostalgic crowd," says Bud, who finds that they are usually the ones who remember black walnuts from their childhood. The walnuts are delightfully pungent, with a strong, delectable aroma. They don't merely blend in with this recipe—they stand out.

Makes 5 dozen

3½ cups all-purpose flour
1 teaspoon baking soda
1 teaspoon cream of tartar
¾ teaspoon salt
1 cup unsalted butter, softened
2 cups lightly packed light brown sugar
2 eggs
2 teaspoons vanilla extract
1 cup coarsely chopped black walnuts

In a medium-size bowl, combine the flour, baking soda, cream of tartar, and salt. In a large mixing bowl, cream together the butter and brown sugar using an electric mixer on medium speed, until light and fluffy, about 5 minutes. Beat in the eggs, one at a time. Add the vanilla. Reduce the speed to low and gradually add the flour mixture. Mix until well blended. Stir in the black walnuts until evenly distributed.

Divide the dough in half and shape each portion into a log about 2 inches in diameter. Wrap in plastic wrap and refrigerate until firm, about 2 hours, or place in the freezer for up to a month.

When ready to bake, preheat the oven to 375°F. Line two cookie sheets with parchment paper. Slice the dough into ¼-inch slices and place 2 inches apart on the baking sheet. Bake for 12 to 15 minutes or until golden brown around the edges. Transfer to a wire rack and let cool completely. Store in an airtight container for up to a week or freeze for up to a month.

Holiday Nut Wedges

Whether you use hazelnuts with their sweet taste and creamy texture, the rich flavor of hicans or pecans, or the bold, earthy tones of walnuts—or a combination of all three—this recipe will surely become one of your top holiday cookie favorites. Easy to make, the flavor and texture is reminiscent of Greek baklava. The sprinkling of coarse sugar adds extra crunch and sweetness.

Makes 16 wedges

1 15-ounce package refrigerated pie crusts (2 crusts per package)
1 cup finely chopped nuts
⅓ cup sugar
2 tablespoons honey
1 teaspoon cinnamon
¼ teaspoon salt
1 teaspoon freshly squeezed lemon juice
Milk or heavy whipping cream, to brush
2 to 3 tablespoons coarse sugar, for sprinkling

Preheat the oven to 375°F. Line a baking sheet with parchment paper. Unroll one of the crusts and transfer to the baking sheet. Set aside.

In a separate bowl, combine the nuts, sugar, honey, cinnamon, salt, and lemon juice. Spread the mixture over the crust to within 1-inch of the edge.

Unroll the remaining crust and place on top. Press the edges to seal and crimp all the way around using a pastry wheel or the tines of a fork. Prick holes over the top of the crust with a fork. Brush lightly with the milk and sprinkle with the coarse sugar.

Bake for 25 to 30 minutes or until the pastry begins to brown. Cool 10 minutes on a wire rack. Divide into wedges while still warm. Cool completely.

PEACE ANGEL GARLIC FARM

Paul Zorn
Morrow, Ohio

The Egyptians worshiped it, the Greeks detested it, the Romans ate it with delight, and Paul Zorn grows it with a passion. Count him among a small but elite group of niche farmers who feed a cook's yen for a singular great ingredient. A whiff and a taste of any one of Paul's naturally grown garlic varieties will make one forever skeptical of the generic varieties stacked in grocery stores which impart the same taste to every recipe calling for its use.

Paul is a full-time employee of the United States Postal Service, with a part-time penchant for farming. From his very small farm, just under three acres, located thirty miles northeast of Cincinnati, he grows and harvests just a little more than an acre of the "stinking rose," an ingredient used in just about every culture and found in almost every kitchen.

Self-taught and a one-man operation, Paul sells a wide variety of naturally grown hardneck and softneck garlic, a list that reads like a United Nations roster: Persian, Russian, Siberian, German, Sicilian, and Korean. Just as distinct as their origin, their tastes are anything but comparable. "Knowing which one to use is kind of like choosing wine," says Paul. "It depends on the person's taste and what you plan to pair it with." Customers need a little Garlic 101, and Paul is a willing instructor. "The rule of thumb when it comes to garlic is the same as choosing chili peppers," says Paul. "The smaller the clove, the hotter." He also coaches on the subtle, and not so subtle, nuances between varieties.

His personal favorite, Persian Star, has pretty, crescent-shaped cloves with lavender stripes tipped in red, and a strong, rich garlic flavor. By contrast, his Russian Heirloom variety called Siberian Rose has creamy cloves and a smooth taste, perfect for roasting. Seoul Sister, a Korean garlic, is sharp, hot, and adds heat to Asian dishes—overuse is a lesson in moderation. Shvelisi, garlic from the Republic of Georgia, has distinct purple stripes and wine-colored cloves, and because it's a hardneck species, resists the urge to sprout.

Paul sells his gourmet garlic, along with fresh berries, from a simple roadside farmstand, only open when there's something fresh to sell. Most of his customers find him through the garlic lover's grapevine, others through the Internet. But the best way to find him, he teases, is to just follow your nose.

Balsamic Roasted Garlic

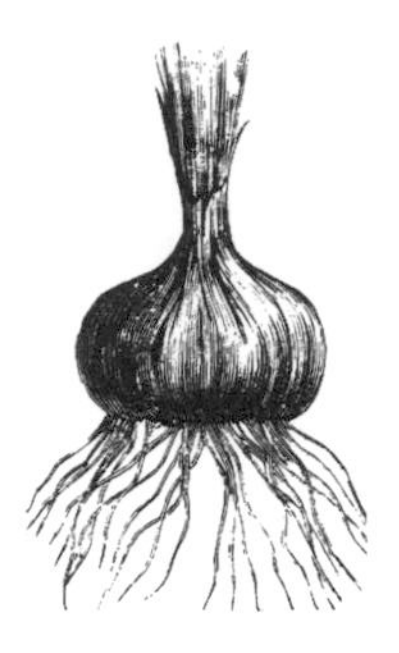

Roasting garlic can make even the most pungent varieties mellow out a bit. It turns the firm cloves into a soft, creamy paste that can be spread on bread, stirred into a soup, or added to dips and vegetables. This version combines garlic, balsamic, and olive oil for a sweet, fruity finish, and the longer cooking time produces wonderful results. The best variety to use is Siberian Rose, which spreads like butter after roasting.

Makes about 1 cup

6 to 8 heads garlic
½ cup extra-virgin olive oil
½ cup balsamic vinegar
1 tablespoon fresh rosemary leaves

Leave the garlic bulbs intact but rub the excess paper skin from the outsides. With a sharp knife, cut about ¼ inch off the tops of the garlic heads to expose the tips of the cloves.

In a small bowl, combine the oil, balsamic vinegar, and rosemary. Place the garlic and the oil mixture in a resealable plastic bag. Seal and allow to sit for 8 hours to marinate, shaking occasionally.

Preheat the oven to 375°F. Remove the garlic from the marinade. Place them, cut side down, in a foil-lined, shallow baking dish. Pour the marinade from the bag into the dish and cover tightly with foil. Bake for 40 to 50 minutes, or until the garlic is soft, squeezable, and fragrant. Remove from the oven and let cool. The garlic should slip easily from the skin when squeezed. Squeeze all the cloves into a bowl and mash with a fork, or work into a paste in the food processor, adding a few tablespoons of oil and a pinch of salt. Store in the refrigerator until needed, for up to a month.

Peace Angel's Linguini Carbonara

When a recipe calls for peeling lots of garlic, here's a suggestion that will make it seem less troublesome: place the separated, unpeeled cloves into a jar with a tight-fitting lid. Shake briskly for about thirty seconds. When you look inside, the cloves will have shed their skins, which will save even more time in preparing this already quick-to-the-table recipe.

Makes 4 servings

2 tablespoons extra-virgin olive oil
1 head garlic, separated into cloves, peeled, and minced
1 teaspoon crushed red pepper flakes
4 cups coarsely chopped fresh spinach leaves
¼ cup chopped fresh basil leaves
1 tablespoon salt
1 pound dried linguini
2 eggs, lightly beaten
1 cup grated fresh Parmesan cheese, plus extra if desired
Salt and freshly ground black pepper

Heat the oil in a large skillet over medium heat. Add the minced garlic and sauté for about a minute, stirring constantly, to soften slightly. Take care not to burn or brown the garlic. Add the crushed red pepper, spinach, and basil leaves, and sauté until the spinach is soft. Set aside.

Bring a large pot of water to a boil and add the salt. Add the pasta and cook 8 to 9 minutes until the pasta is done, yet firm to the bite. Drain, reserving some of the water. Place the pasta back into the pot and cover to keep warm. Warm four dinner plates.

In a separate medium-size bowl, combine the eggs and the cheese. Pour the egg mixture into pasta and toss to combine. (If the pasta appears dry or sticky, toss with a bit of the reserved cooking water until it loosens.) Add the spinach mixture and toss again. Season to taste with salt and pepper. Serve with extra Parmesan, if desired.

Roasted Garlic Spread

Garlic is divided into two categories: softneck and hardneck. Softneck garlic, the typical grocery store variety, has larger, plumper cloves and keeps longer without sprouting, which has a tendency to diminish the flavor of the garlic. Hardneck garlics grow fewer, larger cloves per bulb and what they lack in quantity, they make up for in flavors that range from robust to subtle. A better choice for roasting, try Persian Star or Siberian Rose in this versatile spread.

Makes about 1½ cups

1 head garlic
1 8-ounce package cream cheese, softened
¼ cup milk
½ cup finely chopped scallions
½ cup finely chopped fresh parsley
2 tablespoons dried oregano
2 tablespoons dried thyme
2 tablespoons lemon juice
1 tablespoon extra-virgin olive oil, plus extra
½ teaspoon salt

To roast the garlic: Preheat the oven to 375°F. Remove the loose outer skin from the head of garlic. Do not peel or separate the cloves. Cut ¼ inch off the top of the head so the tips of the cloves are exposed. Drizzle with a little olive oil, wrap in foil, and bake at 375°F for about 40 minutes, or until the garlic is soft when squeezed. Unwrap and let cool.

To make the spread: Squeeze the roasted garlic from their skins into the bowl of a food processor fitted with a steel blade. Add the remaining ingredients and process until smooth. Use to dress-up baked potatoes, as a condiment for sandwich making, or as a spread for bagels.

Garlic Soup with Parsley Spaetzle

Four heads of garlic in a soup may sound daunting but cooking has a way of mellowing the raw flavor and turning it into a sweet sensation. Beware of using spring garlic that has sprouted. The taste is harsh and not enjoyable no matter how long it is cooked.

Makes 8 servings

Garlic broth:

1 tablespoon extra-virgin olive oil
3 or 4 heads garlic, cloves separated, peeled, and coarsely chopped
8 cups vegetable or chicken stock
Salt and freshly ground black pepper

Parsley spaetzle:

2 eggs, lightly beaten
1½ cups all-purpose flour
½ cup water
½ teaspoon salt, plus 1 tablespoon for cooking water
½ teaspoon freshly ground black pepper
¼ teaspoon double-acting baking powder
½ cup chopped fresh parsley or cilantro

To prepare the broth: Heat the oil in a large saucepan over low heat. Stir in the chopped garlic and sauté, stirring often, until the garlic is soft and translucent, not browned. This will take about 20 minutes. Take care to not let the garlic brown. Add the stock and bring to a boil. Reduce the heat to low and simmer, uncovered, for about 45 minutes, or until the garlic is very tender. Season to taste with salt and pepper. Keep warm.

To prepare the spaetzle: Combine all of the spaetzle ingredients in a medium-size bowl. Cover and refrigerate for 1 hour. Meanwhile, bring a large pot of water to a boil. When ready to cook, add a tablespoon of salt to the water. Drop small bits of the batter, about the size of a dime, into the boiling water from a spoon. Cook until the spaetzle are light and delicate, about 5 minutes. Drain. To serve, add the spaetzle to the warm soup.

QUEEN RIGHT COLONIES

Denzil and Shelia St. Clair
Spencer, Ohio

The phone rings at Queen Right Colonies. It's Buzz, a regular customer whose moniker is a perfect complement to his hobby. In a mild panic, Buzz explains that he tried to introduce two Russian queens to his hives but they were rejected by the Italian colonies. Then it really got ugly. The queen's fate was to be covered with propolis while still in the queen cage. The start of the beekeeping season was near and Buzz was in a sticky situation. Always the diplomat, Shelia St. Clair tells Buzz to come right over. She'll help him reseat the throne. Politics play out everywhere, even within the walls of a beehive.

The language spoken among Ohio's almost two thousand beekeepers is a fairly quirky one, filled with obscure phrases and playful words. Denzil and Shelia St. Clair, beekeepers and owners of Queen Right Colonies, a beekeeping supply and honey processing equipment house in Spencer, teach the art and language of beekeeping to more than forty budding apiculturists and hobbyists every year.

The curious name of their business, Queen Right Colonies, means that the queen bee rules the colony with an iron fist and uses her majestic influence to get the job done. Should she need advice, the queen will pipe and quack to get the attention of a queen from the neighboring colony. If the advice is bad and the colony revolts, the queen is kicked out on her stinger.

This is the kind of "sweet talk" Shelia and Denzil have been sharing each of their thirty-five years together. It started with a proposal and a dowry of two colonies from Shelia's grandfather, an avid beekeeper himself. From there, life as beekeepers has evolved into playing host to 150 colonies on twelve acres, collecting and processing anywhere from ten to fifteen thousands pounds of Ohio honey in recent years, defined in taste and color by the flora, herbs, trees, and seasons of northeast Ohio.

Their sophisticated honey palates tell them when it's time to harvest honey collected from a specific nectar source. Denzil's favorite is Black Locust, the first major tree to come into bloom in northeast Ohio. "Bees are bloom specific insects," he explains. "They work the seasons collecting nectar from whatever bloom is prolific until it fades and another kind opens." The big, juicy Black

Locust blossoms are open for business for just two short weeks in late May, just when honeybee colonies reach peak strength. Because bees are fair-weather workers, wet weather or cold spells during bloom often narrows the window of opportunity for collection. It will take the bees at QRC about three weeks to collect and produce thirty pounds of Black Locust honey. Denzil considers this early-season honey to be Ohio's finest table honey, light in color and delicate to the taste buds.

The honeybee is one of man's oldest insect friends, creating the gold standard for many Ohio kitchens. Yet bees work double duty, most important of all fertilizing many of Ohio's crop-bearing plants.

"Other insects do involuntary pollination," says Denzil, "but no other insect can do what a honeybee can to keep other forms of agriculture thriving. Bees can make six to seven hundred trips per day in an apple orchard, or they can fill up on one poppy bloom before returning to the hive," he calculates. "Or they can sap around thirty dandelion blooms." No matter how you do the math, you always come up with one busy bee.

Honeyed Flatbreads

Denzil and Shelia St. Clair's choice for cooking and baking is Black Locust honey. But don't pass up buckwheat honey, which arrives later in the season. Black and strongly flavored, it is another coveted Ohio variety and comes through nicely in this recipe for flatbreads.

Makes eight 3-inch flatbreads

½ cup cottage cheese, drained
3 tablespoons honey
½ teaspoon salt
½ cup all-purpose flour, plus more as needed
Vegetable oil, to grease pan

In a large bowl, combine the cottage cheese, honey, and salt by mashing together with a fork. Add the flour and mix into a dough. The dough will be sticky and slightly bumpy. Turn out onto a floured surface and gently knead in more flour until the dough is no longer sticky but still soft and cool. Cover the dough with plastic wrap and let rest at room temperature for 30 minutes.

Divide the dough into eight pieces. Roll each piece into a thin circle about 3-inches in diameter, about the size of a large pancake. Place a skillet over medium heat and lightly coat with vegetable oil. Cook each flatbread until golden, about 1 minute on each side. Oil the skillet after each use. Serve warm with a drizzle of honey.

Honey and Chive Butter

Three simple yet fresh ingredients make up this sweet butter that's a welcome addition to the table year round. Be sure to use a light-colored honey such as clover or apple blossom that won't overpower other flavors.

Makes about 1¼ cups

1 cup unsalted butter, softened
2 to 3 tablespoons snipped fresh chives or chive blossoms, or a combination
2 to 3 tablespoons honey

Place all the ingredients in a medium bowl. Combine until well blended. Serve with warm, crusty bread. The butter can be refrigerated for up to a week, or frozen for up to three months. Let soften slightly before serving.

WINDY HILL APPLE FARM

Charlie Fritsch
Newark, Ohio

Charlie Fritsch's best customers know where he keeps the "good" stuff. (Hint: It's in the cellar.) Before the first apple ripens in his orchards, his customers begin showing up, empty bottles in hand, walk past the idle cider mill and apple stand to the stairs leading downstairs. That's where Charlie tops off the bottles with hard cider, the color of liquid gold, that has spent the past winter and spring working up a "kick." The bottles are corked, a few dollars exchange hands, and everybody's happy. It's a perfectly legitimate exchange yet there's something about basement-brewed hard cider that feels delightfully naughty.

There was a time when hard cider was the "nip" of choice in Ohio as well as the nation. The legendary Johnny Appleseed scattered apple seeds that flourished into orchards across the state, and English colonists introduced Ohioans to the craft of brewing hard cider, the fermented version of sweet cider. For a few hundred years, hard cider was the toast of the town until beer grew in popularity, the temperance movement gained momentum, and finally prohibition laws were enacted. Hard cider production all across the country dried up, and the process all but died.

A quarter of a century has passed since prohibition laws were lifted but the public's palate for hard cider has been slow to rejuvenate. Today, there are about seventy orchards in Ohio pressing and bottling sweet cider, the family-oriented drink, but Charlie Fritsch's Windy Hill Apple Farm is the only one known to produce and sell hard cider.

Prior to his retirement in 1994 from a career as a mechanical engineer, Charlie planted five acres of disease-resistant apple trees. He watched them grow taller and fuller as he grew closer to devoting all of his time to his apple orchard, where his goal was to raise high-quality apple varieties without the use of chemicals or pesticide residues.

Charlie planted his orchard from left to right beginning with trees whose fruit ripen first in early September: RedFree, JonaFree, Liberty, and Scarlet O'Hara. About two-thirds will be used for eating, pies, and sauces, and the balance will go into making sweet cider. Enough apples will be pressed to produce a thousand gallons of cider blended from multiple apple varieties. Allowed a day's rest before bottling, Charlie's rosy brown-colored cider has a sweet and lively taste descriptive of his orchard.

To the right of the orchard rows are Charlie's "last call" apple trees: Gold Rush and Enterprise. Whether that's a reference to the fact that they are the last to ripen or their destiny as an alcoholic beverage, these are the apples that will be pressed and blended for hard cider. It will take Charlie, and Mother Nature, a little longer to produce hard cider.

The ripe sugary Gold Rush will sit, or "sweat," a couple of months before being pressed. Charlie will blend this juice with that from his Enterprise apples to contribute the necessary tannins for taste, texture, body, and graceful aging. The blend is left to ferment, and the natural sugars begin their conversion to alcohol. The liquid is then racked off, or siphoned, twice over the next few months, when the cider naturally clarifies into a beautiful gold and matures to a 7 percent alcohol content—enough to officially make this an adults-only warm-up for wintery Ohio nights.

Charlie Fritsch makes this hard cider in his basement—and it's delicious. But even those who haven't developed a taste for the drink can raise a glass to his efforts in reviving a deeply rooted tradition in Ohio farming history.

Onion and Cider Soup with Toasted Cheese Croutons

Adding cider to this soup stock creates a sweet balance to the meat stocks and a mellow contrast to the sharp, strong cheese.

Makes 6 servings

Onion and Cider Soup:

3 tablespoons extra-virgin olive oil
3 tablespoons unsalted butter
3 large Spanish onions (do not use sweet varieties), sliced thinly
2 cups apple cider
2 cups chicken stock
2 cups beef stock
Salt and freshly ground black pepper

Cheese Croutons:

6 (1-inch thick) slices French-style bread
Extra-virgin olive oil for brushing
1 cup shredded strong aged cheese, such as Muenster or Gruyére
2 tablespoons chopped fresh parsley
Pinch of cayenne pepper

Place a heavy-bottomed stockpot over medium heat. Combine the oil and butter in the pot, and heat until the butter melts. Add the onions and cook, stirring often, until the onions are soft and browned, about 30 minutes. Add one cup of the apple cider. Turn the heat to high. Allow the liquid to evaporate. Add the remaining cider, beef, and chicken stock. Bring to a boil, then reduce heat to low. Simmer for about 15 minutes. Season with salt and pepper.

Preheat the oven to 375°F. Brush the bread slices with olive oil on both sides. Place in a single layer on a baking sheet. Bake for 10 minutes, or until golden brown. Remove from the oven. Combine cheese, parsley, and cayenne. Top each bread slice with the cheese mixture. Return to oven and bake until the cheese is melted, about 5 minutes.

Ladle the soup into individual bowls. Top each with a toasted cheese crouton. Serve immediately.

Cider Glaze

A basic cider glaze is a versatile addition to a condiment shelf. Add cinnamon and it's a sweet and fruity replacement for maple syrup over a short stack or corn cakes or delicious just mixed with plain yogurt. Scented with savory herbs, such as fresh rosemary or sage, it becomes a finishing glaze for fish, chicken, or pork. Drizzle a few tablespoons over freshly steamed carrots or sweet potatoes, and bring the taste of the orchard to the table all year long.

Makes about 1 cup

4 cups apple cider
¼ cup unsalted butter, diced
1 tablespoon chopped fresh rosemary or sage, for a savory glaze; or 1 tablespoon ground cinnamon, for a sweet glaze

Pour the cider into a medium-size saucepan and bring to a boil. Boil vigorously until the cider reduces to one cup, 20 to 25 minutes. Whisk in the butter. Add the herbs or cinnamon, and blend well. Use immediately, or store, covered, in the refrigerator for up to two weeks. The butter will harden in the sauce. Gently reheat and whisk to emulsify before using.

Thick-cut Pork Chops with Shallots and Hard Cider Sauce

What does hard cider taste like? Although it's not wine, a sip will evoke the same language tossed around at a wine tasting: semidry with a remarkably fresh apple nose, it delivers a crisp, fruit-forward taste and a clean, refreshing finish. A rule of thumb is that hard cider can give pleasure where a white wine might. Pork and chicken, vegetables, and fish can all benefit from a bottle or two of hard cider nearby.

Makes 4 servings

4 (1-inch thick) rib pork chops
Salt and freshly ground black pepper
3 tablespoons unsalted butter, cut into small pieces
4 large shallots, sliced thinly
1 cup hard cider

Preheat oven to 450°F. Pat the pork chops dry and sprinkle both sides with salt and pepper. Melt half the butter in a large, heavy skillet over high heat. Add the chops and brown 6 minutes per side. Transfer to a shallow baking pan and cover to keep warm. Set aside.

Add the shallots and remaining butter to the skillet and cook over medium heat, stirring occasionally, until golden brown and tender, 6 to 8 minutes. Add the cider and boil, stirring and scraping up any brown bits, until reduced to about ¾ cup, about 3 minutes. Season to taste with salt and pepper.

Spoon the shallots and sauce around chops. Place in the oven and bake for about 10 minutes, until an instant-read thermometer inserted horizontally into center of a chop registers 145°F. Let the chops rest for 5 minutes. Spoon the shallots and sauce over the chops and serve.

VINEYARDS & WINERIES

RAISE A GLASS to Ohio vineyards and wineries! You might expect it to be filled with Sparkling Catawba or Concord wine, heritage varietals that are responsible for the solid foundation on which Ohio has built its wine industry. Although the local palate continues to enjoy these historically significant wines from vines introduced in the state almost two hundred years ago, they are no longer the sole definition of Ohio wines. For more than forty years, throughout every winemaking region of the state, from along the shores of Lake Erie through the central plains to the Ohio River Valley, winemakers have been experimenting with vines and producing European-style wines, sometimes in competition with the world's most formidable wine-producing countries but always in harmony with their own surroundings.

Ohio winemakers demonstrate world-class skills and knowledge in the making of fine wines. Ohio Rieslings, Chardonnay, Pinot Gris, Pinot Noir, Cabernet Franc, and Cabernet Sauvignon wines have captured some prestigious medals throughout the world, and the palates of wine lovers from as far away as California.

So what do you pair Ohio wines with? Ohio grown foods, of course!

LAKE ERIE WEST WINE REGION

Claudio Salvador
Firelands Winery
Sandusky, Ohio

Just as a sprinter nervously anticipates the "pop" of the starting gun, a handful of winemakers across the state of Ohio watch and anxiously wait for the thermometer to drop to freezing. When it does, it's the shotgun start for harvesting Vidal Blanc grapes that have clung to the vine purposefully for this moment and exclusively for pressing into ice wine, a unique and wonderfully rich, sweet dessert wine. It's likely the one wine that elevates Ohio's status in the world of wine and puts Ohio winemakers, such as Firelands Winery's Claudio Salvador, in an exclusive class of producers.

Harvesting grapes for ice wine is typically done under dark of night—in one single night. If they're lucky, a full moon will light the vineyards, otherwise headlights from the trucks will do. Vineyard workers work quickly to pluck the frozen clusters, hard as marbles, by hand, load them in crates, and get them back to the winery before the sun comes up and threatens to thaw the harvest.

That's the typical scenario for harvesting ice wine in Ohio, unless it's grapes for Firelands Ice Wine. The sixty-acre vineyards are located on Isle St. George, also known as North Bass Island, the third in a string of islands in the western basin of Lake Erie and eighteen miles offshore from Firelands Winery. The unique microclimate on the island from the still warm lake waters keep the grapes on the vines almost six weeks longer than on the mainland, allowing them to develop complex flavors and sugars for a stellar ice wine.

So when that small window of opportunity opens to collect grapes for ice wine, Claudio and his vineyard workers are ferried over to the island, where they work through the night. By morning, seven or eight tons of grapes are ready to make the trip back to the winery, where they are pressed while still frozen and the water driven out as shards of ice. This leaves a highly concentrated juice, very high in acids, sugars, and aromatics. After a twenty-four hour rest and a slow, cool fermentation process in stainless-steel tanks, the wine develops its intense fruit character, including apricot, peach, and pear flavors. The lively wine is bottled young and meant to be enjoyed that way.

While the uniqueness of ice wine and the drama surrounding its harvest puts the spotlight on such winemakers as Claudio, probably no other winemaker in Ohio better understands the regional palate for sweet heritage wines such as Catawbas, Concords, and Niagaras, which Firelands Winery has been selling and growing since the 1920s under the Mantey Vineyard label. "Heritage wines are the ones which built the foundation for the Ohio wine industry," he says. "But there are a lot more people drinking our Cabernets, Pinot Grigios and Rieslings."

Claudio introduced European vinifera to the Firelands vineyard over twenty-five years ago and continually adds new varieties to test their suitability for Ohio's offshore climate and their potential for making great Ohio grown wine. In 2003, he planted two acres of Dolcetto, a varietal from Italy's Piedmont region, which bears similarities to Merlot, an ongoing challenge for Ohio winemakers, except for its potential for ripening fully before the growing season ends. It's a wait-and-see experience, perhaps a little like anticipating the moment to harvest ice wine.

Ohio Ice Wine Zabaglione

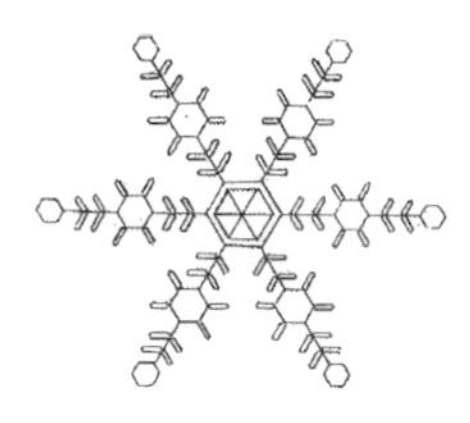

Ice wine is a perfect dessert companion—or a dessert itself. Pour a wine glass only "two fingers" high (about two ounces) and sip along with this classic recipe that features a new twist. Zabaglione is Italian custard traditionally made with Marsala, a rich Italian wine. In this recipe, it takes on the sweet fruity characteristic of the ice wine.

Makes 4 servings

9 egg yolks
¼ cup Ohio Ice Wine
½ cup sugar
4 fresh peaches, peeled, pitted and sliced

Place about 1-inch of water in the bottom pan of a double boiler. Place over medium heat and heat until the water is hot but not boiling. In the upper pan, off the heat, whisk together the egg yolks, wine, and sugar. Place over the hot water. Cook until the egg mixture is heated through but not boiling. Remove from the heat and allow to cool for 5 minutes.

Using an electric mixer, beat the egg mixture for 10 minutes at high speed, or until it has a smooth consistency and a pale yellow color. Serve immediately or refrigerate until ready to use. Serve with sliced fresh peaches and a glass of ice wine.

Walleye with Tomatoes and Black Olives

Claudio Salvador was raised and schooled in the Friuli Venezia Giulia wine region of Italy, characterized by aromatic white wines and austere, dry reds, and where the soil and climate are almost identical to that of his Sandusky winery. For this recipe using Lake Erie walleye, Claudio likes to pair it with an Ohio Pinot Grigio.

Makes 4 servings

4 (6-ounce) walleye filets
4 lemon wedges, to garnish

Marinade:
¼ cup dry white wine
¼ cup extra-virgin olive oil
1 teaspoon chopped fresh Italian parsley

Sauce:
3 tablespoons extra-virgin olive oil
¼ cup chopped onion
2 cloves garlic, minced
2 cups chopped tomatoes, peeled and seeded
¼ cup dry white wine
1 teaspoon chopped fresh oregano
1 teaspoon salt
½ teaspoon freshly ground black pepper
¼ cup kalamata olives, pitted and halved

To prepare the fish: Place the fish in a 9 x 13-inch baking pan. In a medium bowl, combine all the ingredients for the marinade. Pour over the fish and marinate in the refrigerator for 30 minutes.

To prepare the sauce: Heat the oil in a large skillet over medium heat. Add the onion and garlic. Cook until soft and fragrant, 4 to 5 minutes. Add the tomatoes, wine, oregano, salt, and pepper. Cook for 20 minutes, adjusting the heat so the sauce does not boil. Add the olives. Taste and adjust seasonings, if necessary.

Preheat the grill to medium-hot. Lightly oil the grill grate. Remove the walleye filets from the marinade, discarding the leftover marinade. Place on the grate, cover, and grill 4 to 5 minutes per side until the fish flakes easily when tested with a fork. Remove from the grill and place on a large serving platter. Pour the sauce over the fish. Serve with lemon wedges.

OHIO RIVER VALLEY WINE REGION

Ron Barrett and Nancy Bentley
Kinkead Ridge Vineyard and Estate Winery
Ripley, Ohio

When Ron Barrett and Nancy Bentley were dating, he took her to his Oregon vineyard in the Chehalem Valley, where she fell starry-eyed in love with the romance of a vineyard. Nancy, a former New Yorker, had visions of herself strolling through the vineyards, the sun warming her skin, a glass of Pinot Noir in one hand and nibbling grapes straight off the vine with the other. "Somebody forgot to tell me that growing grapes is farming," says Nancy. She soon learned that the forces of nature, predators, unreliable labor, and equipment breakdowns can quickly cloud the quixotic vision of owning a vineyard. Love prevailed and Nancy adjusted. Then Ron decided he needed a change of venue and a new viticultural challenge.

Southwest Ohio topped the list of possibilities, inching out eastern Washington State and southern Oregon. Fertile, unglaciated limestone ridges here mimicked the soil of some of the best grape-growing regions in the world, and the modified continental climate had great potential for fully developed grapes—a mid-September to late October harvest window of cool nights, warm days, and not a lot of precipitation.

Using the Internet, they looked for acreage in the Ohio River Valley appellation, a region initially famous for the American Labrusca variety of Catawba that Nicholas Longworth, father of American wine, used to create. Their first "hit" was an intriguing 1880 Gothic Revival home with beautiful southeast-facing slopes and picturesque views all around. What it lacked in convenience, being far off the roads most traveled, it made up for in its potential for growing fabulous wine grapes. "In New York, the outdoors was the trip from my apartment to the cab," says Nancy. "Now I watch bats fly against the outdoor light, see bluebirds raise their babies in the old cedar fence posts, hear the calls of wild turkey and meadowlarks, and find tiny frogs and beautiful Luna moths."

In 1999, using their best educated guesses, they planted the vineyard with late-maturing wine grape varieties, which ripen slowly into October, producing wines with greater depth and complexity, including Cabernet Sauvignon. They also planted an experimental section with Pinot Blanc, Chardonnay, Semillon, Petit Manseng, Merlot, and Gamay Noir, and have made plans to find additional winter-hardy vines.

In 2001, the first harvest came at Kinkead Ridge without any means to crush the grapes. In the fellowship of making great wine, Andy Troutman of Wolf Creek Winery, himself a new generation of Ohio winemakers, opened his winery in Akron to remedy their dilemma.

The following year, Kinkead Ridge Estate Winery was complete in time for the second harvest of Riesling, Cabernet Sauvignon, Cabernet Franc, Syrah, Sauvignon Blanc, Viognier, Roussanne, and Petit Verdot. They began producing limited quantities of ultra-premium wines, that, in the short history of Kinkead Ridge, have won medals of distinction in several international wine competitions. "During tastings, we'll have visitors who say they only like sweet wines," says Nancy. "After they taste one of our Cabernets made from dead-ripe grapes, they are amazed at how good a dry wine can taste."

Ron and Nancy each have their niche in the process that brings the wine from the vine to the bottle to the customer. As managing partner, her focus is behind the desk: all the marketing and sales, paperwork, and accounting a small business can generate. His focus is on the vineyard, constantly questioning every aspect from the rootstock and grape varieties to the wine yeasts and wine barrels. Nancy says Ron's infinite number of questions couldn't be answered in a lifetime, but his passion has resulted in some extraordinary wines that keep getting better as the vines age.

Pork Tenderloin with Shallots, Grapes, Walnuts, and Rosemary

Makes 4 servings

1 cup orange juice
½ cup walnuts
2 pork tenderloins, about 1 pound each, trimmed of fat
2 tablespoons ground coriander
Salt and freshly ground black pepper
2 tablespoons extra-virgin olive oil
2 shallots, minced
1 cup red seedless grapes, halved
1 tablespoon minced fresh rosemary

Preheat the oven to 350°F. In a small saucepan, boil the orange juice until reduced by half and set aside.

Heat walnuts in a small, non-stick pan over low heat until they are lightly toasted. Remove from heat, cool, and chop coarsely. Set aside.

Rub the tenderloins with the ground coriander, and season with salt and pepper. Heat the olive oil in a large, ovenproof skillet and brown the tenderloins on all sides, about 2 minutes on each side. Place the skillet in the oven and roast for 20 to 30 minutes, until an instant-read thermometer inserted into the thickest part of the tenderloin reaches 145°F. Transfer the tenderloin to a warmed platter, cover with foil, and let rest 15 minutes before slicing.

Place the skillet over medium heat and add the shallots and grapes, sautéing until the shallots are lightly browned and the grapes begin to soften. Add the reduced orange juice and heat until thick and bubbly, about 2 minutes.

Cut the tenderloins into ½-inch thick slices and top with the grape sauce. Sprinkle with the chopped walnuts and rosemary. Serve immediately.

The advantage of operating an estate winery is that a watchful eye is kept on the cultivation, maturing, and harvesting of the grapes. That's a plus for Kinkead Ridge's Cabernet Franc. Nancy Bentley describes its fragrant aromas as those of "violet and black cherry" and the taste as "fruity, harmonious, with chocolate and raspberry overtones," a nice match with this pork tenderloin recipe.

Sautéed Mushroom Medley with Feta on Croutons

Kinkead Ridge has one of the very few Roussanne plantings in the eastern United States. A Rhône blend of aristocratic varieties, this complex and enticing wine has notes of stone fruit and kiwi, and is commonly blended with Viognier, which can be thin. The addition of Roussanne creates a rich mouth feel and is excellent served as an aperitif wine with this savory appetizer.

Makes 4 servings

4 slices bread, crusts trimmed and sliced on the diagonal
2 tablespoons extra-virgin olive oil
½ stick unsalted butter
1 shallot, thinly sliced
3 cloves garlic, minced
1 pound mixed fresh mushrooms (crimini, shiitake, or oyster), sliced
½ cup dry white wine
1 cup crumbled feta cheese (about 5 ounces)
Chopped chives or tarragon, for garnish
Salt and freshly ground black pepper
1 lemon, halved

Heat a large skillet over medium heat. Brush the bread on both sides with the olive oil. Place in the skillet, and brown on both sides. Remove from the skillet and set aside.

In the same skillet, melt the butter over low heat. Add the shallot and garlic, and cook slowly until softened, about 5 minutes. Add the sliced mushrooms and cook until they are soft and release some liquid, about 8 minutes. Slowly add the white wine and continue cooking until almost all the wine has cooked off.

Mound the mushrooms on a warm plate, top with crumbled feta, and sprinkle with chives. Arrange the bread around the mushrooms. Season to taste with salt, pepper, and a squeeze of lemon juice.

LAKE ERIE EAST WINE REGION

Arnulf Esterer
Markko Vineyard
Conneaut, Ohio

In May at Markko Vineyard, the menace of a late frost has safely passed and the tender buds are just beginning to break on the grapevines throughout the fourteen-acre vineyard. Before the season hits full tilt with tours, guests, and filling wine orders, Arnulf "Arnie" Esterer will invite fellow winemakers, vineyard workers, and a host of friends and fans of good wine to gather in a clearing among the vine rows at Markko Vineyard. They'll pause, bow their heads, and ask for the Lord's blessing on every aspect of the season ahead—from an abundance of sunny days balanced by the right measure of rain, to productive vines, healthy workers, and ultimately magnificent wine to be bottled.

Markko Vineyard's annual Blessing of the Vines is an ecumenical celebration based on an old European tradition that Arnie has hosted for over twenty-five years at his winery. It's a day that begins in prayer and song, and ends with a celebration revolving around food and wine in the woods where the winery stands. While Arnie believes there is a higher power accountable for the progression of the vineyard and the results from the cellar, he has spent his forty years as a winemaker elevating Ohio's status as a respected producer of world-class wines.

Formerly an engineer, Arnie is a disciple of Dr. Konstantin Franc, a noted pioneer grower of European wine grapes in the eastern portion of the United States. Beginning in 1969, under Dr. Franc's tutelage, Arnie learned to identify and grow vinifera, or old-world wine grapes that work best in the soil, climate, and growing season along the eastern shoreline of Lake Erie. "Dr. Franc felt that, for Americans to drink the best wines, they had to begin by growing real wine grapes," Arnie explains. "Each region in France and Italy is distinct in soil, climate, and wines and that's what we needed to find here."

Arnie has dedicated himself to marrying rootstock to the soil. For all his efforts, he never attempted to imitate or duplicate a wine grape from another growing region, but sought authenticity in a wine grape that reflected this particular region of Ohio. "If you do everything to manufacture perfect grapes, the taste won't be true to your region," says Arnie. He does not irrigate his vineyard but rather works with nature all season long. One vintage does not duplicate another, so in the end, Arnie plays to the wine, not what the market demands. "Each region in Ohio, or the world for that matter, should focus on what they do best," says Arnie. "That doesn't mean putting limits on what we do, but to narrow the focus."

While geography determines the nuances of how a wine tastes, the raw materials are the grape varieties that go into the wine, and Markko Vineyard's admitted strength is growing white wine grapes. The versatile Chardonnay, which can be grown and ripened in all but the most extreme regions of the world, and Riesling, the noble German variety considered to be beautifully expressive of the region where it's grown, are two varieties that Arnie feels are at home in Ohio and rightfully outshine California's efforts. "Every time someone spends their dollar on one of our wines, or any Ohio wine," says Arnie, "I consider that a vote of confidence for what we are doing."

Markko Vineyard Onion Cake

Germans in the Baden Württemberg and Elsass region welcome the fall with a traditional Zwiebelkuchen, or onion cake. Arnie Esterer of Markko Vineyard pairs the traditional savory cake with his estate Riesling, a varietal that fits naturally into the normal growing season along the eastern shore of Lake Erie.

Makes 12 or more servings

Cake:
2 teaspoons active dry yeast
1½ cups warm water (110°F–115°F)
2 cups all-purpose flour
2 cups semolina flour
1 teaspoon salt
1 tablespoon caraway seeds
2 tablespoons extra-virgin olive oil

Onion topping:
¼ cup extra-virgin olive oil
2 cups chopped onion
3 eggs, lightly beaten
½ cup sour cream
4 slices bacon, cooked and crumbled
½ teaspoon paprika

Prepare the cake: Dissolve the yeast in the water. Set aside. In a large bowl, combine the flours, salt, and caraway seeds. Add the water and olive oil, and mix until a soft dough forms. Transfer to a lightly floured surface and knead until the dough is smooth and elastic, about 10 minutes. Transfer to a lightly oiled bowl, cover, and let rise in a warm place for an hour, or until doubled in size.

Prepare the onion topping: Heat the olive oil in a large skillet over medium heat. Sauté the chopped onion until soft. Remove from the heat and let cool. Add the beaten eggs, sour cream, bacon, and paprika and mix well. Set aside.

Preheat the oven to 400°F. Divide the dough in two portions. Roll each out to a 12-inch circle. Transfer to a baking sheet, cover and let rise for 30 minutes. When dough is slightly risen, divide the onion mixture between the two disks, spreading to the edges. Bake for 20 minutes, or until the topping is lightly browned and the cake is golden. Remove, cool slightly, and serve.

Markko Vineyard Rice Pilaf

Among winemakers, there is often an unrealistic goal to meet the standards of French wines. "We can't and don't want to match those standards," says Arnie Esterer. Instead he finds that wines from along the Lake Erie shore, particularly Chardonnay, are filled with subtle complexities, flavors, and aromas that might not make them a "blockbuster" wine but superior, nonetheless, and meant to be enjoyed with subtly spiced dishes such as this classic pilaf.

Makes 4 servings

2 tablespoons extra-virgin olive oil
¼ cup finely diced shallots
¼ cup finely diced onion
¼ cup finely diced red or green bell pepper
1 cup long-grain rice
½ teaspoon ground cumin
2 teaspoons ground fennel
1 cup chicken or vegetable broth
1 cup dry white wine
½ teaspoon salt
1 teaspoon dried thyme
⅓ cup sliced almonds, toasted
3 tablespoons raisins or currants
2 tablespoons chopped fresh herbs, such as parsley, rosemary, and thyme

Heat the olive oil in a large skillet over medium heat. Add the shallots, onion, and bell peppers and sauté until soft and fragrant, about 7 minutes. Reduce the heat to low, add the rice, cumin, and fennel and stir until the rice is coated with oil and slightly golden, 4 to 5 minutes.

Add the broth, wine, salt, and thyme. Bring to boil and cook, uncovered, for about 5 minutes, until some of the liquid has been absorbed. Cover, reduce heat to low, and simmer for 15 minutes. Remove from the heat and let rest for at least 5 minutes before fluffing with a fork and adding the almonds, raisins, and herbs. Serve warm.

CENTRAL OHIO WINE REGION

Chuck Harris and Nina Busch
Ravenhurst Champagne Cellars
Mount Victory, Ohio

Chuck Harris and Nina Busch describe their lives together as winemakers as "little people doing great things in odd places." There is nothing "little" about these partners in winemaking and marriage. Chuck is a big personality, flamboyant, funny, and quite engaging from behind the tasting bar at Ravenhurst. Nina is a beautiful and rational counterpoint to Chuck's quirkiness. They greet visitors to their winery with a hearty "hello" and get down to the business of how to "taste," not "drink," wine.

Great are the handcrafted still wines bottled under the Busch-Harris label and Ravenhurst champagne produced using old-world methods—many having earned medals in Ohio, California, and American Wine Society competitions. Odd, no doubt, is where the Ravenhurst winery is found. Ten acres of vineyards are planted among endless cornfields in the middle of what might be described as "nowhere," although Chuck likes to think of it as a "destination."

Chuck and Nina's move to Central Ohio was a calculated one, a chance to pursue their passion for country living and good wine. Armed with history and chemistry degrees from Ohio University, they planted vineyards in a region that appeared better suited for growing soybeans and corn. Their hobby grew to over ten acres of vineyard and a commercial winery and tasting room. "We have vines that are over twenty-five years old—an entire generation or more in learning how to grow wine grapes," says Chuck. "Now that it has a history, it helps us to make better wines."

The heavy clay soil caps wonderfully loamy, nutritious soil—four feet down. Vines are planted by augering holes through the thick clay into rich soil. The clay acts as a protective blanket during a harsh winter. Chuck describes the conditions in their vineyard as "Death Valley." In the summer, the soil between the rows forms deep cracks and crevices, stressful conditions for corn and the farmer who grows it, but exciting to the winemaker. "No rain means no rot and little disease to contend with," says Chuck. It also means smaller, sweeter grapes with more intense flavors and heady aromas. That translates into fabulous dessert wines, Pinot Noir with big red raspberry and Bing cherry bouquets, and Chardonnay with lush mango and papaya aromas.

For fear of ending up with even one mediocre wine, Chuck and Nina make wines that "go with what God and the forces of nature give us." "That's how we get our wines to stand out," says Chuck. His philosophy is that if you need the assurance of always having grapes for wine, make wine in California. "If you want to make wine on the edge, come here."

Between 2,500 and 3,000 cases of wine are produced each year from their vineyard, the majority of which goes to Ravenhurst subscribers, dedicated customers who have first dibs on their wines. The remainder will be divided between the winery's retail and tasting room, open only one weekend a month, a few local wine shops, and the Refectory Restaurant and Bistro in Columbus. The thought of expanding the vineyards and winery has crossed their minds—but they prefer to keep the number of people that come between them and the vines to a minimum.

"It was never our intention to make the most wine in Ohio," says Chuck, "just some of the best."

Ravenhurst Aspara-Dogs

It would be safe to assume that this quirky, offbeat recipe is a Chuck Harris original, one that he serves chefs and food professionals who visit the winery. "I can't resist serving this with a flute of Grand Cuvée Champagne—life should always be this much fun!" he says. Use the thickest freshest spears you can find, doubling or tripling up, if needed, to fill the bun.

Makes 6 servings

6 thick spears asparagus, about 5 to 6 inches in length, trimmed and peeled
18 to 24 very thin slices good sugar or maple-cured ham
Stone-ground mustard, to accompany
6 whole-grain hot dog buns
Toothpicks

Wrap each asparagus in three or four slices of ham. Secure with a toothpick. Place in a steamer rack over gently simmering water. Cover and steam for 5 to 7 minutes, or until the asparagus pierces easily with the tip of a knife or toothpick. Remove from the steamer and discard the toothpicks. Place each wrapped spear in a hot dog bun and slather with stone-ground mustard. Enjoy with a glass of Grand Cuvée Champagne.

Nut-Crusted Fish with Peach Tequila Salsa

Chuck Harris has a flair that cannot be denied nor hidden. A winemaker first, his culinary skills run a close second. The salsa that accompanies this delicate nut-crusted fish is steeped in tequila, drained off before serving. Harris considers its consumption a "small reward for a job well done." His choice of wine would be a Busch Harris Chardonnay Reserve, "very complex, very elegant."

Makes 4 servings

Salsa:

2 ripe peaches or pears, peeled and diced
¼ cup diced red onion
¼ teaspoon salt
2 tablespoons tequila

Fish:

½ cup fresh bread crumbs
½ cup finely chopped hickory, hicans or macadamia nuts
¼ teaspoon garlic powder
½ teaspoon salt
¼ teaspoon freshly ground black pepper
¼ cup flour
2 whole eggs, beaten
Dash Tabasco or hot sauce
4 (6 to 8 ounce) walleye, trout or catfish filets
2 tablespoons unsalted butter
2 tablespoons extra-virgin olive oil

To make the salsa: Combine the peaches, onion, salt, and tequila. Mix well and set aside. This can be made 4 hours in advance.

To make the fish: In a shallow bowl, combine the bread crumbs, nuts, garlic powder, salt, and pepper. In a second bowl, place the flour. In a third shallow bowl, combine the eggs and hot sauce. Dredge each filet in the flour, then dip into the egg mixture, and finally dredge in the breadcrumb mixture. Place a large, heavy skillet over medium heat and heat half the butter and oil. Place two of the filets in the skillet and cook about 3 minutes per side, or until the fish flakes easily when tested with a fork. Remove to a platter. Cover to keep warm. Repeat with the remaining butter, oil and filets.

To serve: Drain the tequila from the salsa. Serve the warm filets with a serving of salsa on the side.

Dessert Cherries in Pinot Noir

The cardinal rule for cooking with wine is this: If you won't drink it, don't cook with it. When it comes to deciding which wine to use in a recipe, the rules are just as simple. Use robust reds with red meats and red sauces; dry whites for fish, poultry, pork, and veal; and when preparing regional foods, cook with regional wines such as Busch-Harris Pinot Noir produced at Ravenhurst Champagne Cellars.

Makes 4 servings

1 cup water
½ cup brown sugar, more or less to taste
1 cup Pinot Noir
2 teaspoons lemon zest
1 pound fresh, sweet cherries, washed, stems removed, and pitted

In a medium saucepan, combine the water and brown sugar. Bring to a simmer. Add the wine and lemon zest and return to a simmer. Reduce the heat and simmer for 3 minutes, stirring occasionally.

Add the cherries and return to a simmer for 2 minutes. Remove from heat, cover, and cool to room temperature. If not serving immediately, transfer cherries and liquid to a glass bowl, cover, and refrigerate for up to 2 days.

When ready to serve, spoon the cherries and sauce into small dessert bowls. Serve with a glass of Pinot Noir and tiny sugar cookies.

OHIO HEARTLAND WINE REGION

Andy Troutman
The Winery at Wolf Creek
Norton, Ohio

Andy Troutman calls himself a "fresh face that's been around the vineyards a while." He is undoubtedly one of the youngest winemakers in the state, but when he talks about winemaking, he does so with an air of experience usually reserved for vineyard veterans. When he shares his visions for the Winery at Wolf Creek and the future of Ohio wine production, it's with the energy and enthusiasm of a fresh college graduate, out to shake things up.

After graduating in 1996 from Ohio State University with a degree in agriculture, Andy was making plans to move to California, the epicenter of the American wine industry. A chance meeting with Andrew Wineberg, then owner and vintner at Winery at Wolf Creek just west of Akron, put Andy's plans on hold and placed him in the vineyards for the next couple of years. When Wineberg suddenly died in 2000, Andy stayed on to keep the winery functioning and by then was intrigued and challenged by what Ohio's heartland could produce and had the potential to produce. Andy and his wife, Deanna, purchased the winery in 2002, fulfilling a lifelong dream perhaps a little earlier than planned.

High atop a hill that overlooks Wolf Creek Reservoir and a view of the Akron skyline, Andy points to rows and rows of grapevines, progress he's made in just a few short years. "Eight years ago, I planted Cabernet Franc without knowing what kind of potential it had," he says. Andy calls attention to a ridge in the distance—a continental divide of sorts. It represents the highest elevation in Ohio and puts the winery in its own microclimate, blocking the wind and shedding water to the south. "It gives us all the advantages of Ohio's climate for growing wine grapes including the moderating effects of the lakes and the hot summers, which are good for Cabernet Francs," which unlike their more intense ancestor, Cabernet Sauvignon, are more resistant to cold winters, favor cooler, damp soils, and ripen earlier. Although Andy is still learning the subtleties of growing this variety in Ohio's climate, it's become his favorite to grow and a cause for celebration when it ripens every year.

Perhaps a dreamer and a bit of a risk taker, but not carelessly so, Andy clearly sees the potential in Ohio wines. While other wine growers use Vidal Blanc to make ice wine, Andy still uses it to produce a German-style white table wine. He's experimenting with Müller-Thurgau, a grape widely planted throughout Germany that has a bigger yield than Riesling and ripens earlier. It requires less sun and is undemanding of the climate in which it grows. Could the Ohio winemaker ask for more?

Andy knows there will always be plenty of challenges for Ohio winemakers. "Our biggest challenge is getting people to come down here," he says. "We're not on the 'wine radar.' For a lot of wine lovers, wine means California, Italy, France, and Australia. Our goal is to reach out and invite people into their own backyard."

Grilled Butterflied Leg of Lamb

Cabernet Franc vines bare thinner-skinned, earlier-ripening grapes with lower overall acidity, when compared to their more fragile relative, Cabernet Sauvignon. This red, fruity wine with layers of oak is a good companion for the peppery flavors in the sauce.

Makes 6 to 8 servings

One (4 to 5 pound) leg of lamb, butterflied, trimmed and tied
1 teaspoon coarse salt
1 tablespoon freshly ground black pepper
3 tablespoons extra-virgin olive oil
½ cup dry red wine
10 large garlic cloves, crushed
¼ cup fresh chopped rosemary

Sprinkle both sides of the lamb with the salt and pepper. Combine the olive oil, red wine, garlic, and rosemary. Place the lamb inside a large, resealable plastic bag or a large glass baking dish. Pour the marinade over the lamb, cover, and refrigerate for 8 hours, turning occasionally.

When ready to cook, remove the lamb from the refrigerator and let it sit at room temperature for 1 hour. Brush the grill grates lightly with oil. Preheat the grill to medium-high. Remove the meat from the marinade. Pour the marinade into a small saucepan, bring to a boil, and let boil for 5 minutes.

Place the lamb directly over the fire on the grill and cook for 15 minutes on each side, basting with the marinade. Move the lamb to the side of the grill away from the direct heat and continue to cook for 10 to 15 minutes longer, turning once, or until the internal temperature registers 135°F for medium-rare or 145°F for medium.

Remove the lamb from the grill and cover loosely with foil. Let rest for 10 minutes before carving into thin slices. Serve with Peppered Horseradish Sauce (page 191).

Peppered Horseradish Sauce

The bite and power of horseradish root is virtually undetectable until it is ground or grated. If you choose to grate your own horseradish from fresh root, choose a well ventilated area to complete the task. The potent fumes can quickly clear a room.

Makes 2 cups

½ cup grated horseradish root or prepared horseradish
1 cup hot pepper jelly
¼ cup cider vinegar
1 teaspoon coarsely ground black pepper

Combine the horseradish, pepper jelly, vinegar, and pepper in a bowl and whisk until well blended. Cover and refrigerate until ready to use, for at least 2 hours, although 24 hours is desirable.

Roasted Beet and Spinach Salad

Andy Troutman calls Pinot Gris a "wine in transition," still subject to experimentation both in the vineyard and when it reaches the winery. From season to season, the ripeness at harvest can change the character of this wine greatly—it can be tangy and light or quite rich, round, and full-bodied with pear, honey, and apple character, a nice match for this salad's rich roasted beets, tender greens and tangy cheese.

Makes 6 to 8 servings

1 pound small beets, washed and stems trimmed
1 tablespoon freshly minced shallots
3 tablespoons freshly squeezed lemon juice
½ teaspoon Dijon mustard
¼ cup extra-virgin olive oil
Salt and freshly ground pepper, to taste
4 cups fresh, young spinach leaves, washed and dried
½ cup goat cheese or feta cheese, crumbled
¼ cup walnuts or pecans, toasted and coarsely chopped

Preheat oven to 400°F. Wrap the beets in aluminum foil and roast in center of oven until tender, 45 to 60 minutes. Cool. Peel beets and cut in wedges.

Whisk together shallots, lemon juice, and mustard. Whisk in oil until emulsified and season with salt and pepper. Toss beets in a little dressing.

Divide the spinach between 4 salad plates. Drizzle with the dressing and top with beets, crumbled cheese, and nuts. Serve immediately.

OHIO CHEFS & FARMERS

BETWEEN THOSE WHO GROW FOOD and those who prepare it, a natural connection exists. For the chef, great ingredients, full of flavor, with rich textures and color, are the most important tools of their trade. For the farmers, when a chef features their product on the menu, it's an endorsement, important approval for a job well done. Few can work up the same enthusiasm a chef can over tiny Fairy Tale eggplants, freshly milled grains, or sun-ripened heirloom tomatoes.

Featuring locally grown and raised meats and produce on a restaurant's menu requires commitment from both the chefs and the farmers. It's working with the seasons and Mother Nature, a balancing act between the kitchen and the field. All across the state, farmers and chefs are forging working relationships with something as simple and personal as a handshake, or seeking each other out through organized collaboratives and farm-to-chef networks.

Every time a farmer and chef connect, they help strengthen the regional food economy and opt for better quality on the plate. One bite and the customer will immediately recognize what is at work between the two.

THE CHEF'S GARDEN & CHEZ FRANCOIS

Lee Jones
The Chef's Garden, Huron, Ohio

Chef John D'Amico
Chez Francois, Vermilion, Ohio

Farmer Lee Jones, dressed in crisp business overalls and his signature red bow tie, kicked the mud off his boots and walked into Chez Francois' white-tablecloth dining room. He shook hands with Chef John D'Amico, set up a Bell and Howell slide projector and began to "peddle" the vegetables from his family farm, The Chef's Garden.

Beautiful bunches of rich burgundy amaranth, golden pea tendrils, slender asparagus in soft tones of cream and purple, and brilliant bull's blood beet sprouts filled the projection screen, much larger than their true micro, mini, or petite sizes. From one slide to the next, Jones provided an enthusiastic, unrehearsed narrative that added character and personality to what some dismiss as "just" vegetables. When the lights went up, the chef found the farmer to be a man with a passion for growing a great product. Likewise, the farmer saw the chef as forward thinking, insisting on using only the best ingredients.

Twenty-five years later, Jones now delivers his traveling produce show on a laptop computer, but the pride in his product remains. A sixth-generation farmer on these 210 acres of fertile fields along the Huron River, Jones, along with his father, Bob, and brother, Bobby, once only grew "garden variety" vegetables—tomatoes, zucchini, and cucumbers—selling them off the back of the truck and at the local farmers' market. It took a few, well-nourished relationships with local chefs and food professionals before they started thinking "small."

"A few of our chef customers began asking us to grow vegetables to their specifications, such as baby-size eggplants," said Jones. "We're just 'dumb' farmers—but they were crazy. I mean, who would buy a vegetable before it grew to full size?" Since the customer is always right, they obliged. Chefs ordered up petite squash, tiny tender salad greens specially mixed to suite the chef's palate, and subtly flavored micro herbs barely the size of a thumbnail. Jones began to notice that at every stage of a plant's life it brought something different to the plate.

Chefs from around the world, including Charlie Trotter, Thomas Keller, and

Alain Ducasse, soon regarded The Chef's Garden as the source for artisanal vegetables, grown naturally and slowly to optimize flavor and nutrition—and worthy of a premium price. Their demands created a uniquely satisfying market niche for The Chef's Garden—and thanks to a finely tuned packaging system, the concept of buying local easily stretches far beyond the Ohio state line.

Among the hundreds of varieties of heirloom, antique, and designer vegetables grown at The Chef's Garden, many come from seeds or plants entrusted to the farmer. "We are the humane society for lost and abandoned seeds from all over the world," says Jones. One orphaned plant is Mr. Frye's rhubarb. Bill Frye was a neighboring farmer in Huron who grew sweet, rosy rhubarb and who, long before it was the right thing to do, avoided using chemicals. When his arthritic hands could no longer keep up with the demands of farming, he entrusted his prized plants to Jones, knowing they would be in good hands and good soil. More recently, a Native American chief honored Jones with a handful of ancient corn seeds that the farmer hopes to cultivate, fulfilling the chief's wishes to preserve this small but important part of his heritage. Requests like these are hardly work to Jones. They are an honor.

These are just a few of the stories that Jones passes along to Chef John D'Amico, who shares them with his waitstaff, who then pass them along to Chez Francois customers. Nothing quite enhances the flavors of food like a personal connection from field to plate.

Lobster-Stuffed Erie County Zucchini Blossoms

Chez Francois' chef, John D'Amico, uses the tender early season blossoms, female only, for this fabulous first course that combines the best in French technique and Ohio produce.

Makes 4 servings

8 ounces cooked lobster meat, chopped
1 egg
½ cup fresh bread crumbs
2 tablespoons heavy cream
1 teaspoon chopped garlic
1 teaspoon chopped shallots
1 teaspoon chopped fresh parsley
Salt and freshly ground black pepper
8 zucchini blossoms with baby zucchini attached (see note)
3 tablespoons extra-virgin olive oil
1 cup all-purpose flour
8 sprigs fresh dill, for garnish

Preheat the oven to 350°F. In a large mixing bowl, mix together the lobster, egg, bread crumbs, heavy cream, garlic, shallots, and parsley. Season to taste with salt and pepper. Divide the mixture into eight portions. Open each blossom and make a small slit along the side to open it fuller. Stuff the blossom with the lobster mixture and wrap the blossom around the stuffing.

Place a large, heavy skillet over medium-high heat and heat the olive oil. Dredge the stuffed blossoms in the flour and sauté in the oil until lightly browned on all sides. Transfer to an ovenproof dish and bake for about 5 minutes. To serve, place two blossoms on each plate, top with Dilled Hollandaise Sauce (page 198) and garnish with a sprig of dill.

Note: If you're harvesting zucchini blossoms from your garden, you can tell the female by the thick stem and a small developing squash at the base of the blossom. Cut the blossoms at midday when they are open and full, leaving one inch of stem. Store for up to 2 days in ice water in the refrigerator.

Dilled Hollandaise Sauce

The fresh taste of dill livens this classic sauce. Rich and luxurious, it's about as good as a sauce can get. If the sauce is too thick, it can be thinned by whisking in a little hot water. The same trick will work if the sauce begins to separate.

Makes about ½ cup

3 egg yolks
Juice of ½ lemon
6 tablespoons unsalted butter, melted
1 tablespoon freshly chopped dill
Salt and cayenne pepper

Place about 1-inch of water in the bottom pan of a double boiler. Place over medium heat and heat until the water is barely simmering. In the upper pan, whisk together the egg yolks and lemon juice. Place over the bottom pan of the double boiler and whisk constantly until thick ribbons form. Slowly whisk in the butter. Stir in the chopped dill. Season to taste with salt and cayenne pepper.

Cream of Ohio Corn Soup with Corn Nut-Crusted Scallops

As the harvest changes at the farm, so does the menu at Chez Francois. "We have to change all the time to keep up with the market and meet our customers' expectations that there will always be something new and interesting to cross their plate," says Chef D'Amico.

Makes 4 servings

1 cup heavy cream
1 cup water
4 ears Ohio-grown sweet corn, husked and cleaned, kernels removed from the cob, cobs reserved
1 red bell pepper, stemmed, seeded and roasted
Salt and freshly ground white pepper
2 tablespoons extra-virgin olive oil
2 tablespoons chopped corn nuts or pistachios
4 large fresh sea scallops
2 tablespoons chopped arugula, for garnish

Combine the cream, water, and stripped corn cobs in a large saucepan. Bring to a gentle boil. Cook for 6 to 8 minutes. Strain, reserving the cooking liquid.

Place the corn kernels in a food processor and puree. Return the pureed corn to the saucepan, along with the reserved liquid. Whisk until combined. Season with salt and pepper and keep warm.

Place the roasted red pepper in the food processor and puree. Set aside.

Place a heavy skillet over medium-high heat. Heat the olive oil. Sprinkle the chopped corn nuts onto the sea scallops and sear in the oil for about 1 minute on each side. Remove and set aside.

To assemble the soup, divide the red pepper puree among four shallow bowls. Place a seared scallop on top. Ladle the soup into the bowls. Garnish with chopped arugula.

BOULDER BELT FARM & ALEXANDER HOUSE

Lucy and Eugene Goodman
Boulder Belt Farm, Eaton, Ohio

Chef Steve Friede
Alexander House, Oxford, Ohio

Chef Steve Friede encourages his customers to "taste with their ears." It's not an inherent or even an acquired skill, rather it's listening to the stories behind the plate. It could be about the ingredients or how the dish is prepared—but more often it's about the farmer. Adding a dash of personality to the plate pulls the entire dining experience together from field to fork.

Lucy Goodman is a hardheaded, dedicated farmer with a soft spot for heirloom vegetables and a passion for organic farming. She knocks at the door of Friede's Oxford restaurant, the Alexander House, from spring through fall with an ever-changing seasonal selection of fruits and vegetables—from spring mix to winter squash. Having been on both sides of the restaurant business—a former chef at the Alexander House and now farming nine acres with her husband, Eugene, at Boulder Belt Farm—Lucy knows how to get a chef's attention. "I can tell when the chef is having a bad day," she says from experience. "So if I walk in with something special like tiny Fairy Tale eggplants, I can tell if I've made his day."

Most chefs will agree that the specials featured on a menu are great diversions from the drudgery of the regular menu. "For me, that's when buying from Lucy comes into play," says Chef Friede. "I can't always rely on a steady stream of something being available." (Little things like excessively hot or dry weather seem to get in the way.) "When Lucy shows up with something great, that's my opportunity to get creative." He finds that customers who order the specials are the same ones who like them served with a story on the side.

Chef Steve Friede admits it would be a lot easier to buy from the grocery store or a large distributor that knows no season—and has no story. But he tries to buy local as much as possible. For him, it has nothing to do with distance but everything to do with working with someone you know—like Lucy Goodman.

Alexander House Heirloom Salad

When heirloom tomatoes and haricot verts, or slender green beans, come into season, Chef Friede puts them front and center in this salad. Lucy Goodman likes to contrast the colors and balance the blend of "'maters." Her preference is to mix the old-fashioned Pink Brandywines with the mildly sweet taste of sunny Yellow Taxis, and the Persimmons, huge meaty orange tomatoes with a big flavor.

Makes 6 servings

Vinaigrette:

1 tablespoon sherry vinegar
1 tablespoon balsamic vinegar
1 tablespoon chopped fresh flat-leaf parsley
½ cup extra-virgin olive oil
Salt and freshly ground black pepper

Salad:

¼ pound haricot verts, cleaned and trimmed
2 cups loosely packed arugula, washed and dried
3 pounds heirloom tomatoes (mixed varieties and colors), cut into bite-size pieces
6 ounces aged cheese, such as provolone, thinly shaved

Chill six salad plates. In a small bowl, mix the vinegars and parsley. Whisking constantly, add the olive oil in a thin stream. Season to taste with salt and pepper.

Bring a large pot of salted water to a boil. Fill a large bowl with ice cubes and cold water. Add the haricot verts to the boiling water and cook for 4 minutes, or until crisp-tender. Remove with a strainer and place the beans in the ice water for about 3 minutes to stop the cooking. Remove and drain.

Place the beans, arugula, and tomatoes in a large bowl. Whisk the dressing if it has separated, then pour over the bean mixture, tossing to coat. Divide among the plates and top with shavings of cheese and freshly ground black pepper to taste.

GREENACRES FARM & NECTAR RESTAURANT

Greenacres Farm, Cincinnati, Ohio

Chef Julie Francis
Nectar Restaurant, Cincinnati, Ohio

Chef Julie Francis knows that if she spends just a little more time looking for the freshest ingredients to use in her restaurant's kitchen, she'll spend a lot less time working with them once they arrive at her doorstep. "When you have something great to work with, there's not much you have to do with it," she said. "All I have to do is let the flavors show through."

Owner and chef of Nectar Restaurant, Chef Francis' menu is a showcase of seasonal, locally grown ingredients. One of her best resources is Greenacres Farm where she regularly fills her basket with choice cuts of Black Angus beef, pasture-raised lamb and poultry, fresh eggs, honey, and a variety of heirloom quality produce, all naturally grown and raised with a keen eye on quality and the environment.

Greenacres Farm commands a sprawling six hundred acres throughout the beautiful, upscale Cincinnati suburb of Indian Hill. Yet it blends so harmoniously with the neighborhood and the naturally wooded landscape that for some greater Cincinnatians its existence, just minutes from a Starbucks and a shopping mall, is a welcome distraction.

Over a century ago the scenic tracts were farmed for grain, leaving tired, overworked and nutritionally depleted soil. When community philanthropists Louis and Louise Nippert purchased the property in 1949, they saw great potential in using the rolling acreage to educate future generations about farming, nature, and the environment. So the fields were allowed to remain fallow, gently and naturally retreating to prime grazing land for Black Angus beef cattle raised on chemical-free pasture and an all-natural diet without the use of growth hormones or routine antibiotics. Long before the farm was publicly recognized as an environmentally sensitive, sustainable farm operation, Greenacres operated as such and continues to do so in the hands of a dedicated, focused staff of farmhands, gardeners, and volunteers.

Greenacres Farm shares what they learn with the general public, particularly school-aged children, through environmental, agricultural and cultural arts education centers funded by a private, non-profit operating foundation established in 1988 by the Nipperts. In 1996, the farm began to sell what they raised to the public. Quality-minded chefs like Francis were among the first in line.

On a weekly basis, Chef Francis purchases a variety of cuts processed from the farm's Black Angus beef, a registered herd noted for it's quality of flavor and tenderness—qualities that match an unpretentious cooking style which relies on natural flavors. Whether it's Greenacres ground beef for her haute hamburgers or meaty beef shanks braised in wine and rich beef stock, her efforts to spend a little more time shopping for great ingredients are a benefit to her, her customers, and the local farms.

"It connects everyone," she says, "providing a sense of community between the farm, and the chef, and the people we both feed."

Braised Beef Shanks

Beef shanks are some of the toughest yet most flavorful cuts of beef. Chef Julie Francis uses a long, slow braising technique as part of this trilogy of recipes that creates the perfect and complete supper on a winter's day.

Makes 4 servings

4 tablespoons unsalted butter, divided
2 tablespoons extra-virgin olive oil, divided
3 stalks celery, diced
1 large onion, diced
3 carrots, scraped clean and diced
4 meaty beef shanks, ½ pound each, cut 1½ inches thick
Salt and freshly ground black pepper, to season
Flour to dust shanks
1½ cups red wine
2 cups beef or veal stock
5 cloves garlic, peeled and crushed
¼ cup tomato paste
6 sprigs each fresh thyme, parsley, and rosemary
2 fresh bay leaves

Preheat the oven to 325°F. Place a large roasting pan over medium heat. Add half the butter and half the oil. Add the celery, onion, and carrots and sauté 8 to 10 minutes or until soft. Remove from pan and keep warm.

Season the shanks with salt and pepper. Dust with flour to coat. Add remaining oil and butter to the pan. Brown the shanks on all sides, 2 minutes per side. Remove from the pan and keep warm.

Add the wine, stock, garlic, and tomato paste to the pan, scraping up any browned bits from the bottom. Bundle the herbs together with butcher twine and add to the pan along with the beef shanks, vegetables and water to cover by ½ inch. Cover and place in oven. Cook for 3 hours or until shanks are fork tender.

Remove shanks from pan and keep warm. Skim off excess fat from the braising liquid and turn the heat to high to reduce until liquid is slightly thickened, about 10 minutes. Serve shanks with Horseradish Mashed Potatoes (page 205) and Roasted Root Vegetables (page 206).

Horseradish Mashed Potatoes

The tang of the horseradish is beautifully tempered by the rich deep flavor of Braised Beef Shanks (page 204). Don't skip the step of drying the potatoes in the oven. It's the magic step when looking for a fluffy texture in mashed potatoes.

Makes 4 servings

4 medium Yukon Gold Potatoes, scrubbed clean and unpeeled
1 tablespoon salt
1 cup heavy cream
3 to 4 tablespoons fresh ground horseradish
4 tablespoons unsalted butter
Salt and freshly ground black pepper

Heat the oven to 350°F. Place potatoes in a large pot. Add water to cover along with the tablespoon of salt. Bring to a boil, then reduce to simmer and cook until potatoes pierce easily with a fork, about 25 to 30 minutes. Drain and arrange on a baking sheet. Place in the oven for 10 to 12 minutes to dry slightly.

Meanwhile, combine the cream, horseradish and butter in a medium saucepan and warm over low heat. Remove the potatoes from the oven. Peel and place in a large bowl with the horseradish mixture and mash until smooth. Season to taste with salt and pepper.

Roasted Root Vegetables

Roasting gives these unassuming, dusty root vegetables a crusty exterior, a creamy interior, and heightened flavor. Simply adorned with some salt and pepper, they are perfect next to roasted or braised meats.

Makes 4 servings

8 small beets, scrubbed and trimmed of greens
12 baby carrots, peeled and tops trimmed
12 baby parsnips, peeled and tops trimmed
4 tablespoons extra-virgin olive oil
Salt and freshly ground black pepper

Preheat the oven to 375°F. Toss the beets with half the olive oil and season with salt and pepper. Toss the carrots and parsnips with the remaining olive oil and season with salt and pepper. Spread on a rimmed baking sheet and roast for 30 to 35 minutes until tender. Slip skins from beets, if desired, and serve.

KING FAMILY FARM & CASA NUEVA

J. B. King
King Family Farm, Albany, Ohio

Chef Thom Herbe
Casa Nueva, Athens, Ohio

It takes J. B. King six months to raise his York Hampshire hog breeds to a meaty 250 pounds on a barnyard meal of roasted soybeans and signature mix of corn, oats, and minerals. Antibiotics and growth hormones are not on their menu. The way J. B. feeds and cares for his hogs will translate straight to the plate through rich meaty cuts that earn enthusiastic nods from customers in the dining room and the kitchen.

To get the reaction he's looking for, J. B. nurtures working relationships with over twenty-five Athens and Columbus-area restaurants. They taste, listen, and understand that J. B. puts a lot of pride and ownership into raising his hogs. "It changed their opinion of the farmer and what our job is—if they know me, they know my product," says J. B. "It has also changed our opinion of chefs."

The first, most dedicated, and longest lasting union King forged was with Casa Nueva, a well-established, worker-owned Athens eatery where the focus is on fresh, wholesome, and local foods. The Mexican-inspired menu at Casa Nueva emphasizes seasonal produce, meats and poultry, herbs, maple syrup, and breads from over twenty-five local farms and producers, including pork from the King Family Farm. J.B. King walked into Casa Nueva in 2001 with just a couple of slabs of his lean premium bacon and some specialty cuts. These days, he unloads more than eighty pounds of pork cuts every week, from ground pork and tenderloins, to shoulders, ham, and bacon.

"When we began buying local, it was grateful retribution for the community and farmer support—not bank support—we received when we were starting up," said Tom Herbe, chef and partner of Casa Nueva. "The bonus is that we get to work with food that passes from field to plate quickly—the freshest possible."

J. B. King raises up to a thousand hogs a year, with over a third going to his faithful list of restaurant accounts. King freely admits that his pork costs more than what a restaurant could procure through a food service distributor, and that's a challenge. But to compare the quality of the two would hardly be comparing apples to apples.

Chorizo Albondigas

"Let's face it," says Chef Thom Herbe, "a beautiful product grown or raised in another part of the country gets increasingly less attractive as it makes its way to Ohio, both in appearance and ethic. The only way to avoid the lag between the producer and the customer is to get it within driving distance of the restaurant." Barely ten miles down the road from Casa Nueva puts J. B. King in the right place!

Makes 4 servings

1 pound ground pork
½ teaspoon black pepper
1 teaspoon dried oregano
1 teaspoon garlic powder
1 teaspoon paprika
½ teaspoon salt
1 teaspoon chili powder
½ teaspoon cayenne pepper
3 tablespoons cider or malt vinegar
¼ cup dry bread crumbs
¼ cup grated Parmesan cheese
4 cups hot cooked rice
1 cup prepared sweet, smoky barbecue sauce, warmed
¼ cup chopped scallions

Preheat oven to 425°F. Place the ground pork, seasonings, vinegar, bread crumbs, and cheese in a large bowl. Mix until well incorporated. Roll into sixteen one-inch balls and place in a shallow baking dish. Bake for about 15 minutes, or until done. Remove from the dish and drain on paper towels. Divide the rice and meatballs among four plates. Top with the barbecue sauce, chopped scallions, and serve.

RAINFRESH HARVEST & NORTHSTAR CAFÉ

Barry Adler
RainFresh Harvest, Plain City, Ohio

Kevin & Katy Malhame, Owners
Northstar Café, Columbus, Ohio

Twenty-two miles of road comes between RainFresh Harvest and Northstar Café. Sounds far but when it comes to philosophy on how good food should come to the plate, this restaurant owner and farmer couldn't be closer.

Barry Adler, owner of RainFresh Harvest, farms a fruit orchard, solar greenhouse for herbs, micro and salad greens, blackberries, and red raspberries on nine acres. He uses what nature provides in "green energy," through the sun and wind, to heat his greenhouse and power equipment. He adheres to "green growing" methods, such as organic composting, to grow great ingredients.

Kevin and Katy Malhame, co-owners of Northstar Café in the trendy Short North of the capital city, count on the collective wisdom of a partnership they have formed. More than a dozen like-minded individuals work together to run a sustainable and energy efficient kitchen using organic and naturally raised foods, the majority of which come from small farms like Barry's within driving distance of the café. The Malhame's are among a new breed of Ohio restaurateurs embracing classic culinary thinking, that is, great food begins with great ingredients. To get the café's philosophy across, each managing partner is required to spend some time working on one of the farms that supply ingredients. "They take part in planting, harvesting and really getting their hands dirty," says Kevin, "and they come away with a better understanding about the connection between the field and the kitchen."

Barry and the partners at Northstar meet regularly to do a little menu and crop planning. They count on Barry as a reliable source for the primary ingredient in Northstar's Sweet Basil Burrito or for leafy bunches of peppery flat-leaf parsley for Parsley Buttermilk Biscuits, tender baby arugula, and more. As the harvest on his farm progresses, Barry keeps Northstar in season by always letting them know when the crisp Asian pears from his orchard are at their peak or when the red raspberries are full and fragrant. That's when, and only when, these ingredients appear on the menu, because as Malhame sees it, "Some foods are not meant to travel far."

On a typical day, the line at the Northstar Café winds out the door and onto the street around the noon hour. That sight alone makes Barry proud to be a part of the food experience at the café. As for the Malhames, who take pride in their commitment to supporting the local farmer, customers willing to wait is the ultimate compliment.

Northstar Café's Parsley Buttermilk Biscuits

When it came to parsley, Barry Adler considered the green a bland personality in the world of herbs. "I didn't think it was anything more than window dressing for the plate," he admits. That's until he tasted these parsley-laced biscuits which revealed, of all things, taste! Clean and peppery, parsley can indeed hold its own in a recipe.

Makes 16 to 18 biscuits

3½ cups all-purpose flour
3½ teaspoons baking powder
1 teaspoon baking soda
1 teaspoon salt
1 cup cold unsalted butter, cut into ½-inch dice
1 cup buttermilk
1 cup minced fresh flat-leaf parsley, washed and dried

Preheat oven to 375°F.

In a large bowl, combine the flour, baking powder, baking soda, and salt. Add the butter and work it into the dry ingredients with a pastry blender or your hands until the mixture resembles a coarse meal.

Add the buttermilk and parsley, and mix until just combined. Transfer the dough to a floured surface, and press or roll into a rectangle about ¾-inch thick. Using a cookie or biscuit cutter, cut out 2-inch rounds. Transfer the biscuits to a baking sheet and bake for 15 to 18 minutes, until slightly golden on top. Remove and let stand 10 minutes before serving with creamery butter or parsley.

Caramelized Onion and Sage Frittata

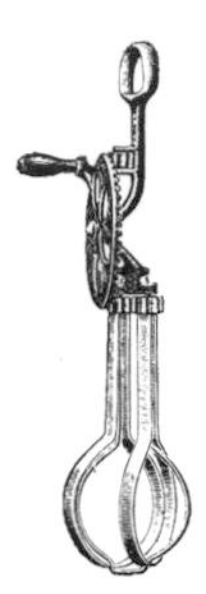

Barry Adler defers to chefs when it comes to culinary uses for herbs, —and chefs leave it in Barry's hands to get the freshest herbs to their kitchen door. When this savory breakfast or brunch item is on the menu, Adler will harvest bunches of sage in the cool morning hours, just after the dew evaporates, triple-rinsing and delivering them for use the next morning. Really fresh sage will have a musty mint taste and add a heady aroma.

Makes 6 to 8 servings

4 tablespoons unsalted butter
1 large onion, thinly sliced
12 eggs, lightly beaten
½ cup minced fresh sage
1 cup freshly grated buttery cheese, such as Gouda or Havarti
Salt and freshly ground black pepper

Preheat the oven to 350°F.

Place a large ovenproof skillet over medium heat. Melt the butter and let it heat until it becomes foamy. Add the onion and cook, stirring often, until soft and caramelized, 15 to 20 minutes. Reduce the heat to low, add the eggs and sage, and cook uncovered for 5 minutes or until the bottom of the frittata is set. Sprinkle with the cheese, and season to taste with salt and pepper.

Place in the oven and bake for 10 to 15 minutes, until the frittata is set and the center wiggles slightly. Remove and let sit for 10 minutes before slicing.

STICKY PETE'S MAPLE SYRUP & VILLAGE BAKERY

Laura McManus
Sticky Pete's Maple Syrup, Athens, Ohio

Chef Christine Hughes
Village Bakery, Athens, Ohio

Chef Christine Hughes buys 80 percent of the fresh and seasonal ingredients for her café and bakeshop, Village Bakery, from local sources. She's quick to point out that she's not looking for just "farmers." She's looking for food artisans—growers and producers who take personal care in how they grow or raise their products.

On one wall in the east room of her sunny café, you'll find a map of southern Ohio, pinpointing all who supply products and ingredients that go into her breakfast and lunch menus and bakery. A network of thin ribbons stretch from Village Bakery, located just outside the Ohio University campus, to farms within fifty miles. Turn around, and the shelves behind are stocked with locally made gourmet sauces, butter, pestos, pastas, and more.

Amid the lattice of ribbons is one pink strand that connects Village Bakery to Sticky Pete's Maple Syrup and Laura McManus. Petite and personable, Laura and her late husband, John, named the two-hundred-acre maple forest after a lovable Husky-mix stray who was notorious for getting into sticky situations.

When the maple-sugaring season begins at the end of February, more than a thousand taps begin to flow and Laura, an energetic one-woman operation, will bottle anywhere between two hundred and four hundred gallons of syrup. She'll sell every last drop of the amber-colored syrup with a significant portion going to Village Bakery, where it is used as one of the primary sweeteners.

The relationship between the two women entrepreneurs works. They genuinely like each other and respect the other's work. Some days a warm hug, instead of a handshake, between the two is a welcome component in the sometimes gritty, often demanding businesses of farming and running a successful restaurant.

For Laura, the idea of selling her product locally isn't measured in miles, but in the sense of community it creates. "I put a lot of TLC into producing my maple syrup, and my chef customers, like Christine, know I love what I do," she says. "I would like to think it comes through in the taste."

Village Bakery Maple-Smoked BBQ Sauce

For cooks who love a challenge, Chef Christine Hughes obliges with this wonderful barbecue sauce that gets sweetness and body from real maple syrup. For this recipe, you'll need a heavy Dutch oven or large pot with a tight-fitting lid, and an inexpensive steamer basket that will be used for stovetop smoking only. Don't be tempted to skip the step of smoking the onions. It's quick, simple, and adds a smoky layer to the sauce.

Makes about 2 quarts

1 cup smoking wood chips, such as hickory or maple
2 large onions, peeled and quartered
2 tablespoons safflower or canola oil
½ tablespoon salt
6 cloves garlic, peeled and crushed
1 teaspoon cayenne pepper, or more to taste
5 pounds fresh meaty tomatoes, peeled and seeded
¾ cup real maple syrup
¾ cup apple cider vinegar
½ tablespoon vanilla extract
½ cup extra-virgin olive oil

Line a heavy-bottomed pot with a tight-fitting lid with a layer of heavy-duty aluminum foil. Place it over a medium-low flame. Put the wood chips in the bottom and place a steamer basket with the onions over the woodchips. Cover with another piece of foil and place the lid on top. Smoke the onions for 30 to 40 minutes. The onions should be light brown. Remove and let cool.

Place a large stockpot over medium heat and sauté the onions in the oil with half the salt until translucent. Add the garlic and cayenne pepper, and sauté for another 5 minutes. Add the tomatoes and cook for 30 minutes, stirring often. Lower the heat and add the maple syrup and vinegar. Cook, uncovered, for 2 to 3 hours to thicken the sauce. Adjust seasonings, adding salt if needed.

Remove from the heat and add the vanilla and olive oil. Set aside to cool. Puree in batches in a food processor or blender. Refrigerate for up to one month or divide into batches and freeze for up to 6 months.

STUTZMAN FARMS & SWEET MOSAIC

Monroe Stutzman
Stutzman Farms, Millersburg, Ohio

Chef Heather Haviland
Sweet Mosaic, Cleveland, Ohio

Chef Heather Haviland stands in the middle of the shed where Amish farmer Monroe Stutzman has his grain mill. It's a curious invention created from an assortment of hoses, fan belts, funnels, old bottles, sifting screens, buckets, and a host of nuts and bolts. At full tilt, the diesel-powered contraption is very loud, delivering a dramatic and wildly entertaining performance that shakes the room. As this is happening, you forget that wheat goes into a hopper at one end and emerges as a beautiful, silky flour at the other.

The Tremont pastry chef uses Stutzman's grain and flours for the breads and pastries served at Sweet Mosaic, her neighborhood bakery and café. Witnessing the laborious process that takes grain from field to flour puts a new spin on why she seeks out these local sources for great ingredients.

About a third of Stutzman's 180-acre Holmes County dairy farm is used for growing organic wheat, oats, corn, and spelt, an ancient grain with a mellow, nutty flavor. Spelt has slowly been gaining culinary popularity. But because spelt has a smaller yield per acre than wheat and requires more processing to make flour, some farmers can't be bothered. Not Monroe.

Abiding by Amish traditions, the young Monroe won't farm with the help some modern technologies might afford. So he opts to farm in ways that suit him and benefit his customers—organically, hands on, and with attention to detail.

Demand for all of Monroe's wonderful grain products is growing. With help from family and community, a new building has been raised to house a bigger, newer diesel-powered mill with the potential for processing more grain a little faster and a little more efficiently. Eventually the new mill will silence the pieced together mill.

"I can tell that Monroe loves what he does," says Chef Haviland. "He respects the earth, takes care to raise his grain the right way, and works hard to achieve a great finished product. And when you taste that freshly milled flour in breads—well, it reminds me of why I go that extra step to find farmers like him."

Multigrain Apple Pecan Scones

More spelt is grown in Ohio than any other state in the nation, a fact that puts farmer Monroe Stutzman, who relies on old-world methods to farm, on the cutting edge of this culinary trend. The grain is showing promise as a flour substitute for those on gluten-free diets.

Makes 8 to 12 scones

1 cup all-purpose flour
⅓ cup whole wheat flour
1¼ cups rolled oats
¾ cup rolled spelt
¾ cup firmly packed brown sugar
¼ teaspoon grated nutmeg
1 tablespoon baking powder
½ teaspoon baking soda
1 teaspoon salt
1 tablespoon ground cinnamon
½ cup coarsely chopped pecans
¾ cup unsalted butter, diced and chilled
2 medium Granny Smith apples, peeled, cored, cut into small chunks, and frozen for one hour
¾ cup buttermilk (no substitutes), plus extra for brushing
½ cup cinnamon sugar, for sprinkling

Combine the dry ingredients and pecans in a large mixing bowl. Cut in the butter until the mixture appears coarse and crumbly. Add the frozen apple pieces and the buttermilk and stir until just combined.

Turn the mixture out onto a lightly floured surface and divide into two parts. With floured hands, shape each piece into a disk about 5 inches across, tapering the edges. The dough will be soft and sticky.

Place the disks onto a parchment paper-lined cookie sheet and place in the freezer for 30 minutes. Remove and cut each disc into four or six wedges. Do not separate wedges. Brush with buttermilk and sprinkle with cinnamon sugar. Bake at 350°F for 35 to 40 minutes or until golden brown.

Italian Corn Cookies

Freshly milled cornmeal gives this special pressed cookie a distinctive character. Adjust the fabulously gritty texture to your liking by using fine, medium, or coarse grind cornmeal.

Makes about 3 dozen cookies

½ cup unsalted butter, room temperature
¼ cup sugar
1 egg
1 teaspoon vanilla extract
¾ cup all-purpose flour
½ cup medium grind cornmeal
¼ teaspoon salt
¼ cup white sesame seeds or coarse sugar, for sprinkling

Preheat the oven to 325°F. In a large bowl and using an electric mixer, cream the butter and sugar together until light and fluffy, 4 to 5 minutes. Scrape down the sides of the bowl and add the egg and vanilla. Mix until incorporated. Add the flour, cornmeal, and salt. Mix until incorporated. Do not chill the dough.

Place the dough into a cookie press fitted with a pinwheel or flower disk. Press onto an ungreased cookie sheet. Sprinkle with sesame seeds or coarse sugar. Bake for 15 to 20 minutes, or until golden brown.

SAVE A FARM

Maier Family Farm
Fred and Carol Maier
Atwater, Ohio

It was difficult to decide whether to put Fred Maier's story at the beginning or end of this book. To place it here seems a natural finale, an exclamation point of sorts, for it to follow the stories told of just a fraction of the small family farms found throughout Ohio.

Fred, a skilled woodworker, farms twenty acres in Portage County, raising Shetland sheep primarily for spinning fleece, breeding stock, and a little freezer lamb. His primary crop, however, is the cultivation of thought.

For a number of years, Fred was involved in farmland preservation at the county level. He watched as Ohio's small, independent farms surrendered to the rising costs of land, labor, and fuel and dealt with profits that couldn't stay ahead of costs. Competition from factory farms and foreign suppliers systematically squeezed out the little guy. An aging farm population, lacking a strong legacy of successors, slowly found themselves wondering who would inherit the family farm.

Farmland all across the country was dwindling at a rate of six acres a day. Fred did the math and realized that all of the farms in Portage County, including his own picturesque niche, would be gone by 2035, swallowed up by housing developments, parking lots, or shopping centers, or left to lay dormant. "I don't know if that will happen," he admits, "but the prospect is shocking."

So Fred got busy planting the seeds of suggestion. Along a few well-traveled country roads, which run throughout Portage County, he has planted rows of spirited rhymes in the style of the infamous Burma Shave jingles, one of the most memorable advertising campaigns in America. Instead of touting a clean shave, the last line reminds the reader to "Save a Farm."

Songs once sang of soap
Old Burma Shave praised
We sing now in hope
That farms not be razed
SAVE A FARM

Winter's on its way
But it will not stay
Spring will follow soon
We'll be back in June
SAVE A FARM

Old MacDonald had a cow
Old MacDonald had a pig
...or once he did!
Now the yellow 'dozers dig
SAVE A FARM

Warm weather's here again
Our signs are back, too
Their jingles all bring
One message to you
SAVE A FARM

Carrots from out west
Greens and all the rest
Import them? Why, oh?
Grow 'em in Ohio
SAVE A FARM

Fred received a telephone call from one motorist who had noticed the catchy jingles. "What can I do to save a farm?" she asked excitedly. And that's precisely how the effort to Save a Farm begins—with one person's desire to do more.

It's hard to measure whether Fred's message to save a farm—any and every farm—is getting across, without any real methods in place to track consumer response or sales made as a direct result of the signage. Yet in that one breathless and eager response, it was clear to Fred that someone was paying attention.

WHAT CAN YOU DO TO SAVE A FARM?

• **EVERY CHANCE YOU GET, BUY LOCALLY.** Share the wonderful tastes with your family, friends, and neighbors and tell them where you bought it. The success of local growers depends on you spreading the word about what they are doing.

• **COOK, CAN, AND FREEZE LOCAL PRODUCTS.** It not only extends the taste of the season well into the winter months, it's another opportunity to eat locally all year round. Imagine how wonderful field-ripened Ohio raspberries, strawberries, or tomatoes will taste when the winter winds blow!

• **GET CHILDREN INVOLVED.** It's never too early to educate Ohio's youth about the great tastes from their own backyard. Visit orchards and farms that encourage you to "pick-your-own." When you get home, help them prepare some simple recipes that highlight the just-picked flavors.

• **PAY ATTENTION TO LAND-USE ISSUES.** Educate yourself about what's happening to the land in your neighborhood or community.

• **ASK QUESTIONS.** Inquire of your local government or regional planning commissions about their plans to preserve agriculture. Ask what they are doing to protect open spaces.

• **TALK TO FARMERS.** Go straight to the source to find out what you can do to help save a farm. Get to know the person who grows or raises your food. Once you do, that peach you bite into or the chicken you roast for your family will never taste the same.

For more information, be sure to visit www.saveafarm.org.

RESOURCES

Point-of-Sale Definitions

On-site: Retail store or roadside stand located at the farm; open year round or seasonally
Farmers' Markets: Area farmers' markets held off-site; call farm for locations
Retail Outlets: Various retail sites around the state; call for locations
Sales from web site: Ordering direct from the Internet
Telephone sales: Call ahead to order
Direct to restaurants: Custom orders for chefs

It's always recommended to call ahead for more information or before visiting.

EGGS, MILK, AND CHEESE

BREYCHAKS BLUE EGG FARM
26140 Akins Road
Columbia Station, OH 44028
(440) 667-0551
www.breychak.com
On-site

BUCKEYE GROVE FARM &
BUCKEYE GROVE FARM CHEESE
50543 Run Road
Beallsville, Ohio 43716
(877) 926-1904
www.buckeyegrovefarmcheese.com
On-site; farmers' market; sales from the Website

HARTZLER FAMILY DAIRY
5454 Cleveland Road (Rt. 3)
Wooster, OH 44691
(330) 345-8190
www.hartzlerfamilydairy.com
On-site; various retail outlets

LARKSONG FARM
8940 County Road 235
Fredericksburg, OH 44627
(330) 695-4581(voice mail)
Sold under the Organic Valley label

MEATS AND POULTRY

ROSE RIDGE FARM
7055 Largo Road
Malvern, Ohio 44644
(330) 904-5365
Farmers' market

FORREST FAMILY FARM
4124 Hamilton Richmond Road
Oxford, Ohio 45056
(513) 523-1387
On-site; telephone sales

J & K JACOBS
150 North First Street
Hamler, OH 43527
(419) 274-1089
Retail outlets

KING FAMILY FARM
3940 Factory Road
Albany, OH 45710
(740) 698-3940
www.kingfamilyfarm.com
Retail outlets; direct to restaurants

SPECKLED HEN FARM
5675 County Road 23
Cardington, OH 43315
(419) 768-2279
www.speckledhenfarm.com/home.html
Farmers market; retail outlets

PRODUCE

BOULDER BELT FARM
P.O. Box 593
3257 U.S. 127N
Eaton, OH 45320
(937) 456-9724
www.boulderbeltfarm.com
CSA membership; on-site; farmers' market; direct to restaurants

BRAMBLE CREEK FARMS
257 Old River Road
Little Hocking, OH 45742
(740) 989-0334
www.bramblecreekfarms.com
Farmers' market; direct to restaurants; on-site

BRIDGMAN FARM
5411 State Route 753
Washington Court House, OH 43160
(740) 335-5410
Farmers' market; direct to restaurants; on-site

THE CHEF'S GARDEN
9009 Huron-Avery Road
Huron, OH 44839
(800) 289-4644
www.chefs-garden.com
Direct to restaurants only

GREENACRES FARM
8255 Spooky Hollow Road
Cincinnati, OH 45242
(513) 891-4227
www.green-acres.org
On-site; direct to restaurants

INTEGRATION ACRES
160 Cherry Ridge Road
Albany, OH 45710
(740) 698-6060
www.integrationacres.com
Farmers' market

JUST THIS FARM
7657 Feder Road
Galloway, OH 43119
(614) 853-1036
Farmers' market; on-site; direct to restaurants

KILLBUCK VALLEY MUSHROOMS, Ltd.
7927 Overton Road
Burbank, OH 44214
(419) 846-3258
Direct to restaurants; farmers' market

MULBERRY CREEK HERB FARM
3312 Bogart Road
Huron, OH 44839
(419) 433-6126
www.mulberrycreek.com
On-site

OASIS ACRES
2429 Paradise Road
Orrville, OH 44667
(330) 683-8199
Farmers' market; direct to restaurants; on-site

OHIO APPLE GROWERS
Local orchard locator
www.ohioapples.org

PEACE ANGEL GARLIC FARM
416 West Pike Street
Morrow, OH 45152
(513) 899-4463
www.peaceangelfarm.com
On-site; sales from Website

RAINFRESH HARVESTS
9559 Industrial Parkway
Plain City, OH 43064
(614) 738-9559
www.rainfreshharvests.com
Direct to restaurants; retail outlets

RICH GARDENS ORGANIC FARM
385 King Road
Shade, OH 45776
(740) 696-1301
Farmers' market

SAGE'S APPLES
11355 Chardon Road
Chardon, OH 44024
(440) 286-3416
www.sagesapples.com
On-site

SCHULTZ FRUIT FARM
7192 Brooklane Road
Chesterland, OH 44026
(440) 729-7447
On-site; farmers' market; direct to restaurants

SHAFER'S PRODUCE
16524 State Route 568
Findlay, OH 45840
(419) 423-0232
On-site

SIPPEL FAMILY FARM
6398 State Route 19
Mount Gilead, OH 43338
(419) 946-1394
CSA membership; farmers' market; direct to restaurants

THE ORCHARDS OF BILL & VICKY THOMAS
2230 Irish Ridge Road
Philo, OH 43771
(740) 674-6814
www.cabinintheorchard.com
On-site; farmers' market

WINDY HILL APPLE FARM
1740 Sportsman Club Road
Newark, OH 43055
(740) 587-3632
www.windyhillapplefarm.com
On-site; farmers' market

FISH AND SEAFOOD

FRESHWATER FARMS OF OHIO, Inc.
2624 North U.S. Highway 68
Urbana, OH 43078
(800) 634-7434
www.fwfarms.com
On-site

POLLY'S PRAWNS & POLLY'S FLOWER FARM
3375 Factory Road
Albany, OH 45710
(740) 589-2326
On-site annual sale; direct to restaurants; retail outlets; farmers' market

VINEYARDS AND WINERIES

FIRELANDS WINERY
917 Bardshar Rd.
Sandusky, OH 44870
(419) 625-5474
(800) 548-WINE
www.firelandswinery.com
On-site; retail outlets

KINKEAD RIDGE VINEYARD AND ESTATE WINERY
904 Hamburg Street
Ripley, OH 45167
(937) 392-6077
www.kinkeadridge.com
Sales from Website; local wineshops

MARKKO VINEYARD
4500 South Ridge Road
Conneaut, OH 44030
(800) 252-3197
www.markko.com
On-site; sales from Website, telephone orders

RAVENHURST CHAMPAGNE CELLARS
34477 Shertzer Road
Mount Victory, OH 43340
(937) 354-5151
Sales from Website; local wineshops

OHIO WINE PRODUCERS ASSOCIATION
33 Tegam Way
Geneva, OH 44041
(800) 227-6972
www.ohiowines.org

THE WINERY AT WOLF CREEK
2637 South Cleve-Mass Road
Norton, OH 44203
(800) 436-0426
www.wineryatwolfcreek.com
On-site; retail outlets

RESTAURANTS

The following is a partial list of restaurants in the state that make a purported effort to buy from local growers.

ALEXANDER HOUSE
22 North College Avenue
Oxford, OH 45056
(513) 523-1200

CASA NUEVA
6 West State Street
Athens, OH 45701
(740) 592-2016 (Restaurant)
www.casanueva.com

CHEZ FRANCOIS
555 Main Street
Vermilion, OH 44089
(440) 967-0630
www.chezfrancois.com

NECTAR
1000 Delta Avenue
Cincinnati, OH 45208
(513) 929-0525
www.thenectarrestaurant.com

THE NORTHSTAR CAFÉ
951 North High Street
Columbus, OH 43201
(614) 298-9999
www.thenorthstarcafe.com

SWEET MOSAIC, Inc.
777 Starkweather Avenue
Cleveland, OH 44113
(216) 374-9030
www.sweetmosaic.com

VILLAGE BAKERY & CAFÉ
268 East State Street
Athens, OH 45701
(740) 594-7311
www.thevillagebakerycafe.com

MAPLE SYRUP

FRANKLIN'S TALL TIMBERS
3459 Jefferson Road
Ashtabula, OH 44004
(440) 812-5784
On-site; retail outlets

OHIO MAPLE SYRUP PRODUCERS ASSOCIATION
1680 Madison Avenue
Wooster, OH 44691
(419) 869-7353
www.ohiomapleproducers.com

STICKY PETE'S PURE MAPLE SYRUP
18216 South Canaan Road
Athens, OHO 45701
(740) 662-2726
On-site; direct to restaurants

GRAIN PRODUCTS

STUTZMAN FARMS
6197 Township Road 605
Millersburg, OH 44654
(330) 828-8454
On-site; farmers' market

HONEY

QUEEN RIGHT COLONIES
43655 State Route 162
Spencer, OH 44275
(440) 647-2602
On-site

NUT ORCHARDS

LUERS NUT FARM
5312 Possum Run Road
Bellville, OH 44813
(419) 892-2043
On-site; telephone sales

OHIO NUT GROWERS
ASSOCIATION
5977 Dalton Fox Road
North Lawrence, OH 44666
www.onga.org

OHIO COOKING SCHOOLS

The following is a partial list of cooking schools in the state that make a purported effort to buy from local growers.

THE CULINARY VEGETABLE
INSTITUTE
12304 Mudbrook Road
Milan, OH 44846
(419) 499-7500
www.culinaryvegetableinstitute.com

LAUREL RUN COOKING SCHOOL
2600 North Ridge Road
Vermilion, OH 44089
(440) 984-5727
www.laurelruncookingschool.com

THE LORETTA PAGANINI
SCHOOL OF COOKING
8613 Mayfield Road
Chesterland, OH 44026
(440) 729-1110
(888) 748-4063
www.lpscinc.com

MUSTARD SEED MARKET & CAFÉ
3885 West Market Street
Akron, OH 44333
(330) 666-7333
www.mustardseedmarket.com

WESTERN RESERVE
SCHOOL OF COOKING
140 North Main Street
Hudson, OH 44236
(330) 650-1665
www.wrsoc.com

SAVE A FARM

THE MAIER FARM
4695 Bassett Road
Atwater, OH 44201
(330) 325-0238
www.saveafarm.org
Grain Products

ADDITIONAL AGRICULTURAL RESOURCES THROUGHOUT THE STATE OF OHIO

OHIO ECOLOGICAL FOOD AND FARM ASSOCIATION
P.O. Box 82234
Columbus, OH 43202
(614) 421-2022
www.oeffa.com
Dedicated to promoting and supporting sustainable, ecological, and healthful food systems. Consumers guide and growers information.

INNOVATIVE FARMERS OF OHIO
P.O. Box 854
Logan, OH 43138
www.ifoh.org
Networking organization of farmers and producers across the state; includes central Ohio chef grower network.

FARM AID
11 Ward Street, Suite 200
Somerville, MA 02143
(800) FARM-AID
www.farmaid.org
Locate family farmed food.

EAT WILD
29428 129th Avenue SW
Vashon, WA 98070
www.eatwild.com
Online source for safe, healthy, natural, and nutritious grass-fed beef, lamb, goats, bison, poultry, and dairy products.

OUR OHIO
Ohio Farm Bureau Federation, Inc.
280 Plaza, P.O. Box 182383
Columbus, OH 43218-2383
(614) 249-2400
www.ourohio.org
Consumers guides and directories to purchasing locally produced food, plants, flowers, agriculture-related entertainment, and more. Lists of agriculture related events for consumers and farmers.

FOOD ROUTES NETWORK
P.O. Box 55-35 Apple Lane
Arnot, PA 16911
(570) 638-3608
www.foodroutes.org
Food Routes "Find Good Food" map can help you connect with local farmers, CSAs, and local markets near you.

LOCAL HARVEST
220 21st Ave
Santa Cruz, CA 95062
(831) 475-8150
www.localharvest.org
Use this Website to find farmers' markets, family farms, and other sources of sustainably grown food in your area, where you can buy produce, grass-fed meats, and many other goodies.

THE NEW FARM
www.newfarm.org
Online guide to the global community of food producers, plus resources for crop and livestock production, local food systems, and more.

BIBLIOGRAPHY

Gentile, Roger. **Discovering Ohio Wines.** Canal Winchester, OH, Enthea Press, 1991.

Gorman, Michelle. "The Persevering Pawpaw: A Native Fruit Regains Popularity," **Ohio Woodland Journal,** April 7, 2005.

Herbst, Sharon Tyler. **Food Lover's Companion: Third Edition.** New York: Barron's Educational Series, 2001.

Johnson, Hugh and Jancis Robinson. **World Atlas of Wine, 5th Edition**. London: Octopus Publishing, 2001.

National Turkey Federation, 1225 New York Avenue NW, Suite 400, Washington, DC.

Schneider, Elizabeth. **Vegetables: From Amaranth to Zucchini.** New York: William Morrow, 2001.

Sharp, Jeff S. "Ohioans Views of Agriculture & Local Foods," Ohio Survey Core Project of the SRI (Social Responsibility Initiative), The Ohio State University, OARDC Extension, March 3, 2007.

RECIPE CREDITS

Hot Milk Cake from The Hartzler Family, Wooster, OH

Big Blueberry Muffins adapted from a recipe from the Ritz Carlton Cookbook

Beer-Braised Lamb Shanks; Corn Spoonbread; Mustard and Herb Crusted Rack of Lamb Reprinted with permission from The American Lamb Board

Italian Leg of Lamb; Greek Lamb Stew from Nick and Kathy Forrest, Oxford, OH

Heritage Dressing from Carol Kosik, Vermilion, OH

Cider-Braised Chicken from Carla Snyder, Western Reserve School of Cooking, Hudson, OH

Raspberry Tart in a Nut Crust from Mary Deucher, Wakeman, OH

Asparagus With Tomatoes, Shallots, and Pistachios from Christina Matijasic, Vermilion, OH

Sweet, Hot, and Tangy Barbecue Sauce Reprinted with permission from Integration Acres, Albany, OH

Pawpaw Lassi Reprinted with permission from Casa Nueva, Athens, OH

Shiitake and Black Walnut Stuffing; Sautéed Oyster Mushrooms and Fingerling Potato Salad from Killbuck Valley Mushrooms, Burbank, OH

Aunt Jane's Black Walnut Refrigerator Cookies from Meredith Deeds, Western Reserve School of Cooking, Hudson, OH

Heirloom Spaghetti Sauce; Japanese Eggplant Spread; Rainbow Salt Potatoes from Lisa Sippel, Mt. Gilead, OH

Lavender Roasted Vegetables from Karen Langan, Mulberry Creek Herb Farm, Huron, OH

Ohio Ice Wine Zabaglione; Walleye with Tomatoes and Black Olives from Loretta Paganini, The Loretta Paganini School of Cooking, Chesterland, OH

Pork Tenderloin With Shallots, Grapes, Walnuts, and Rosemary; Sautéed Mushroom Medley with Feta on Croutons from Kinkead Ridge Vineyard and Estate Winery, Ripley, OH

Grilled Butterflied Leg of Lamb with Peppered Horseradish Sauce from Bev Shaffer, Mustard Seed Market, Akron, OH

Markko Vineyard Onion Cake; Markko Vineyard Rice Pilaf from Arnulf Esterer, Markko Vineyards, Conneaut, OH

Ravenhurst Aspara Dogs; Nut-Crusted Fish With Peach Tequila Sauce from Chuck Harris, Ravenhurst Champagne Cellars, Mount Victory, OH

Lobster Stuffed Erie County Zucchini Blossoms with Dilled Hollandaise Sauce; Cream of Ohio Corn Soup with Corn Nut-Crusted Scallops from Chef John D'Amico, Chez Francois Restaurant, Vermilion, OH

Alexander House Heirloom Salad from Chef Steve Friede, Alexander House, Oxford, OH

RECIPE CREDITS

Chorizo Albondigas from Casa Nueva, Athens, OH

Braised Beef Shanks; Horseradish Mashed Potatoes; Roasted Root Vegetables from Chef Julie Francis, Nectar Restaurant, Cincinnati, OH

Parsley Buttermilk Biscuits; Caramelized Onion Frittata from Northstar Café, Columbus, OH

Maple-Smoked BBQ Sauce from Chef Christine Hughes, Village Bakery, Athens, OH

Multigrained Apple Pecan Scones; Italian Corn Cookies from Chef Heather Haviland, Sweet Mosaic, Cleveland, OH

PHOTO CREDITS

Photography by Marilou Suszko with the following exceptions:

Page 21, Photo courtesy of Hartzler Family Dairy, Wooster, OH. Photo by Judy Fitzpatrick

Page 72, Photo by Yoon, Athens, OH

Page 87, Photo by Mary C. Bridgman, Washington Courthouse, OH

Page 137, Photo courtesy of Ron Franklin, Jefferson, OH

Page 142, Photo by Warren Taylor, Albany, OH

Page 164, Photo courtesy of Charles A. Fritsch, Newark, OH

Pages 171 and 179, Photos courtesy of Ohio Wine Producers Association, Geneva, OH

Page 194, Photo courtesy of The Chef's Garden, Milan, OH

Page 218, Photo courtesy of Fred and Carol Maier, Atwater, OH

Inside Back Cover, Photo by David Deucher, Vermilion, OH

RECIPE INDEX

C

L

M

R

S